THE GREATEST MYSTERIES OF THE
UNEXPLAINED

THE GREATEST MYSTERIES OF THE
UNEXPLAINED

A COMPELLING COLLECTION OF THE WORLD'S MOST PERPLEXING PHENOMENA

LUCY DONCASTER
AND ANDREW HOLLAND

PICTURE CREDITS:

Getty Images: 8 Terry Fincher/Stringer, 13 Topical Press Agency/Getty Images, 22 Bettmann, 25 Michael Ochs Archives/Stringer, 41 Pierre Verdy, 83 Keystone/Stringer, 103 Topical Press Agency/Stringer, 114 Horace Bristol/Stringer, 132, 153 Three Lions/Stringer, 156, 167 Leonard McCombe/The LIFE Images Collection, 203 Topical Press Agency/Stringer, 205, 216 Hulton Archive/Staff, 227 Bob Gomel/Contributor, 240 Neil Armstrong/Stringer.

Naval Historical Center: 30

This edition published in 2021 by Arcturus Publishing Limited
26/27 Bickels Yard, 151–153 Bermondsey Street,
London SE1 3HA

AD007727UK

Printed in the UK

CONTENTS

DISAPPEARANCES

Every day, all over the world, people go missing – either of their own volition, or due to circumstances beyond their control. When a person in the public eye disappears, such as Lord Lucan or Agatha Christie, the case grips the public imagination, with sightings of the missing person being reported from all quarters. Speculation about the motivation behind these events rages, although the truth of the matter is often never discovered.

When an area has a history of repeated vanishings, such as the Bermuda Triangle, the possibility of some sort of extra-terrestrial intervention inspires fevered speculation. But disappearances of any sort leave unsolved mysteries and unanswered questions.

LORD LUCAN

The disappearance of Lord Lucan has perplexed the nation and confounded the law for decades. There are many unanswered questions concerning the crimes from which he fled and, 30 years later, the mystery is no nearer to being solved.

Until the time of his vanishing, Lord Lucan lived the life of a typical English aristocrat. After leaving boarding school, he embarked upon a short career in the armed forces. This was followed by a brief stint in merchant banking before he turned his hand to his main passion in life – gambling. In this, he displayed an obvious affinity with risk-taking. In fact, he enjoyed such success that he earned himself the nickname of 'Lucky', and, to the consternation of his wife, took up gambling as a profession.

Lord Lucan and his fiancée Veronica Duncan photographed on the announcement of their engagement in October 1963.

However, as time went on, Lucan's luck appeared to change and he accrued a large tally of gambling debts that threatened the financial security of his children. It was this, together with other factors, which led to the breakdown of his marriage and the ensuing bitter custody battle between the estranged couple.

On 7 November 1974, matters went from bad to worse. In Lucan's family home in London, two crimes took place – the murder of the children's nanny, Sandra Rivett, and the attempted murder of his wife. Accounts of the events which took place on this night vary as much as the many theories that attempt to explain what happened. However, the identity of the prime suspect for both of these crimes is something upon which all seemed to agree – Lord Lucan himself.

After the crimes took place, Lucan gave his own personal account to friends. He stated that an assailant had entered the house and brutally attacked his wife, leaving her hysterical and bleeding profusely. Lucan had interrupted the assault and wrestled with the attacker, slipping during the struggle in the blood that covered the floor. Realizing that he had thus unwittingly implicated himself in the attack, he reasoned that he would have difficulty in proving his innocence, and decided to flee.

In opposition to this is the report given by Lady Lucan, which was supported by an inquiry. In this, she claimed that Lucan had intended to murder her that night, but that the attempt had gone wrong and he had killed the nanny by mistake. Lady Lucan stated that she herself had fought with her ex-husband, and had been lucky to escape with her life. Her injuries appeared to support this story, but was her assailant actually her husband?

A third theory that has been put forward is that Lucan had hired a hit man to kill his wife, but that the supposed assassin had mistakenly murdered Sandra Rivett instead, as the two women were of a similar build. Lucan then attempted to dispose of Rivett's body, but on being disturbed by his wife had tried to murder her, in line with the original plan.

Many believe that the fact that Lucan fled the scene of the crime and abandoned his distressed wife is proof of his culpability. Since Lucan's disappearance, there have been many unofficial reported sightings of this elusive fugitive all over the world. This has served only to deepen the sense of mystery surrounding this particular case, and it seems likely that unless he surfaces, the truth of the crime and how he managed to vanish without trace may never be known.

AGATHA CHRISTIE

It is somehow fitting that Agatha Christie, the undisputed queen of mystery writing, should have been involved in her own mysterious event – her sudden, unexplained disappearance. Although only temporary, this occurrence has never been properly explained. What were the reasons behind the event, which could easily have come straight out of one of her own elaborate murder stories?

Christie disappeared on the evening of Friday, 3 December 1926. When asked by the police to provide an alibi, her husband Archie was forced to admit that he had spent the weekend with his mistress. This information led police to suspect that Archie may have had a motive for murder, or that she may have taken her own life.

A wide-ranging search began immediately and, the next day, her abandoned car was discovered, strewn with her clothes and belongings. The vehicle was located near both a quarry and a lake, fuelling suspicion that Christie may have committed suicide. Coincidentally, the lake had actually featured in one of her crime novels as the site of a drowning. In light of these factors, the police had the lake dredged, but they found nothing.

The search was then widened to the surrounding countryside, with thousands of volunteers drafted in. This also proved fruitless. Then, after a few days of press publicity, Christie was identified as being alive and well in a health spa in Yorkshire, where she was staying under an assumed name.

The official explanation was that Christie had been suffering from amnesia, brought on by the death of her mother. This, however, sounded

Agatha Christie in around 1926, a few months before her mysterious disappearance.

more like a fabrication than anything grounded in reality, and the public remained mystified.

Christie never revealed her actions or motives to anyone, and as she died in 1976, it is unlikely that we shall ever know the truth. She made no mention of the episode in her memoirs and, whenever asked about her disappearance, she never wavered from the amnesia story.

Over the years, there has been much speculation about the possible reasons for what happened. Could it have been an act of revenge on Christie's adulterous husband, or the symptoms of a nervous breakdown, or even a cleverly constructed publicity stunt? Whatever the reasons, the event can only enhance her reputation as a true mistress of the unexplained.

DR LEON THEREMIN

The peculiar disappearance of the scientist and inventor Dr Leon Theremin is thought to have more to do with the shady world of international espionage than with any other possible cause. It seems likely that Theremin vanished in order to work for the Kremlin and thus further the Soviet cause, but whether this was of his own choosing, or whether he was coerced into doing so, is a matter for speculation.

Dr Theremin arrived in the USA in 1927, bearing his original Russian name, Lev Segeivitch Terman. His particular area of expertise was radio electronics, and it did not take him long to put these skills to commercial use. After spending some time working on a revolutionary musical instrument, he successfully obtained a patent for it, and it became known as the 'Theremin'. The way in which this strange instrument is played is totally unprecedented, since sounds are created by moving the hands around two radio antennae rather than by any physical contact with the machine.

The eerie notes emitted by this instrument resulted in its use in a number of films of the time, including those of Alfred Hitchcock, in which the sounds were used to create suspense. The effect of this was to raise Dr

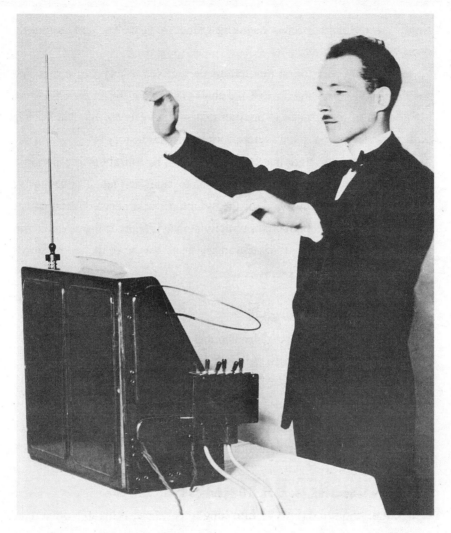

Leon Theremin playing his revolutionary musical instrument.

Theremin's public profile and he began to enjoy a kind of celebrity status in the USA. This fame, however, may have proved to be a double-edged sword, as whilst Theremin enjoyed the fruits of his success, those with sinister intentions became aware of how this talented scientist could assist them in their schemes and plans.

It was Theremin's experiments in the field of radio waves and frequencies, and subsequent creation of the first radio surveillance 'bug', which are thought to have sealed his fate. In 1938 the inventor went missing, and after a while he was presumed to be dead.

It eventually transpired that Theremin had left his house in 1938 in the company of several Soviet agents, who accompanied him back to his homeland. Here, he was thought to have worked for the Soviets on espionage devices and security systems. It is unclear whether or not he was in fact kidnapped, but it seems unlikely that he would have voluntarily exchanged his successful life in New York for the Siberian labour camp in which he ended up.

Many questions about this intelligent man remain unanswered. Was Theremin really interested in using his skills to further the demands of the Cold War powers? This seems unlikely and, although trained in the field of science, when given the choice, Theremin applied himself instead to the peaceful development of music.

Theremin's unexplained disappearance was one of the many curious incidents that have since been attributed to the Soviet authorities during the Cold War. The incredible paranoia and secrecy of that period has left many lasting mysteries. Only now, years after the era ended, are we finding even small clues as to the truth of what actually went on at that time.

THE VANISHED BATTALION

When a person disappears, a range of possible reasons for what has happened spring to mind. Did the missing person suffer some kind of mental breakdown? Did they take their own life? Or could they even have been kidnapped? These are the most obvious explanations. When, however, a large number of people vanish together, without trace, the usual assumptions become less valid.

When a group of people disappears on land, rather than in the air or at sea, the occurrence becomes even more perplexing. The sea will always hold a certain mystique and is easily capable of hiding the evidence if lives have been lost there. This is much harder to do on land, however, and it is thus truly remarkable that, in 1915, no fewer than 250 British soldiers and 16 officers simply disappeared from a battlefield in the Dardanelles region of Turkey.

Although well known for its scrupulous record keeping, the military was, and is, unable to shed any light on what might have happened. Furthermore, the strong adherence to the laws that prevent desertion would seem to preclude the idea of these men trying to escape their duties. It is very unlikely that more than a few of the officers spoke the local language, and anyone captured deserting would have been shot as an example to others. In addition to this, the men who disappeared were formed from the staff of the king's Sandringham estate. Undoubtedly, this would have been a source of great honour to them and not something that they would have discarded lightly.

The men in question had formed E company of the Fifth Territorial Battalion of the Royal Norfolk Regiment, which had been formed in 1908 at the personal behest of King Edward VII. More informally, however, the soldiers were known as 'The Sandringhams'. These men would all have known each other well, both through their work on the estate and due to the fact that they had all grown up together in the same area.

Prior to the outbreak of war, the company consisted of just over 100 part-time territorial soldiers, but after hostilities began more men from the area joined up voluntarily. In those days, military rank would have been decided by social class rather than on any martial merit, with the members of the local gentry forming the ranks of officers. The middle-ranking soldiers, the non-commissioned officers (NCOs), would have been chosen from workers such as the butlers, foremen and gamekeepers, while the rank and file of the troops would have consisted of the labourers and servants from the royal estate.

Despite their lack of experience, the men were keen to engage with the enemy and, after their initial training, they were taken to Turkey to participate in the battle at Gallipoli. They were led into this first engagement by their commanding officer, Colonel Horace Proctor Beauchamp, who would have been eager for his company to make its name on the battlefield.

The last sighting of the missing men occurred on 12 August 1915, just two days after they had arrived at the conflict. They had been given the order to advance on a position that was held by the Turks about 2km (1.2 miles) away. The position was well defended and they had to attack in broad daylight with little in the way of cover. As the troops advanced, Colonel Beauchamp led from the front and harried his men to press the assault. The soldiers are believed to have driven ahead further than the rest of the main assault and may have become cut off from them. They were last sighted entering some woods near the Turkish position, in disarray, and obscured by smoke and clouds.

When the battle was over it was realized that the entire group of men was missing. Despite the horrendous rate of casualties in the First World War, it was unusual for there to be no survivors at all. Enquiries were made to ascertain whether any of them were being held in Turkish prisoner-of-war camps, but this was proven not to be the case. How, then, could this many men have simply disappeared, literally, in a cloud of smoke?

It is possible that the reason behind the battalion's disappearance lies within the realms of the paranormal? In 1965, at the fiftieth anniversary of the fateful Gallipoli landings, a former New Zealand sapper, Frederick Reichardt, claimed that he had witnessed a strange event that could explain what had happened. This account was supported by three other veterans, who all asserted that something out of the ordinary had taken place on the battlefield.

Reichardt stated that he and his fellow soldiers had witnessed the Sandringhams' heroic charge into the woods, whereupon they seemed to rush headlong into a peculiar formation of about eight loaf-shaped clouds which were lying at ground level over the area. The soldiers were seen to enter the clouds, but never appeared again. Reichardt states that, after about an hour, the clouds rose up into the sky, leaving no trace of the soldiers of the Norfolk battalion.

Whether this explanation has any basis in reality is open to speculation.

There are some who would argue that perhaps some kind of religious intervention had taken place. This was the battalion's first engagement, and so none of them had yet been bloodied by the carnage. Perhaps they had been spirited away to heaven before they had had a chance to become sullied by the horrors of war.

Others view the story of the clouds as evidence of an extra-terrestrial abduction. This seems to tie in with some of the descriptions given when ships and aircraft disappear, as they often vanish into cloudy skies. It should be remembered, however, that heavy clouds are an indication of poor weather conditions, which could explain the disappearances.

A third suggestion is that the clouds seen on the battlefield were not due to atmospheric conditions at all, but were in fact palls of smoke emanating from the intense fire and bombardment of the battlefield. As such, then, the soldiers had not disappeared at all, but had simply been killed. This seems unlikely, however, as there are very few military engagements in which where there are no survivors whatsoever.

A fourth and final possibility is believed by many historians to be the most likely explanation, although perhaps this is because they are unwilling to countenance some of the other, more unusual, theories. The suggestion put forward is linked to the brutal reputation of the battalion's Turkish opponents, who were renowned for taking no prisoners. If they did happen to hold any soldiers captive, it was usually only for a very brief period, before they then executed them en masse. In support of this theory, a large number of corpses was found buried on the battlefield in the following years, with execution-style gunshot wounds to the head. Could the peculiar disappearance of all these men be attributed simply to a mass murder?

Similar crimes had been committed before on the battlefield, as history will attest. It is entirely possible that the Turks may have found themselves threatened by the sheer numbers of their own captives, and thus may have executed the men for their own safety.

Although the disappearance of these men is shrouded in mystery, it is certainly not the only occasion on which soldiers of the Great War have gone missing in action. The incredible levels of carnage on the battlefields of Europe meant that many thousands of men remained unaccounted for after battle, with bodies rendered unrecognizable due to the scale of the bloodshed. What sets this mystery apart from others, however, is the fact that all the men vanished together, never to be heard of again. It is a mystery that has perplexed historians for generations, and will no doubt continue to do so until some breakthrough evidence is found.

D. B. COOPER

The disappearance of D. B. Cooper on 24 November 1971 is an interesting tale. This criminal managed to evade the law after hijacking a commercial airliner and then parachuting from it into oblivion, taking with him a large sum of money that he had received as a ransom payment.

What remains a mystery is how Cooper ever managed to escape from the vast operation mounted to secure his capture. The area in which his parachute would have come down is a huge, remote forest that was covered with a thick blanket of snow at the time. More than 300 Federal Bureau of Investigation (FBI) agents spent over a month combing the area for any evidence of Cooper, but none was ever found.

The hijacking of aircraft was a remarkably common occurrence between 1967 and 1972, with more than 150 taking place during this period. Generally, however, hijacks were carried out for political motives. Cooper was the first person to exploit the weakness of air security for his own financial gain.

In planning the operation, Cooper had been particular about his choice of aircraft, ensuring that the one he boarded was a Boeing 727. The reason for this was that the 727 was the only passenger airliner with steps that lowered from a hatch at the very rear of the aircraft, beneath the tail. This hatch would allow Cooper to make his daring escape by parachute. Later, all 727s were modified to prevent such an attempt being made again.

Cooper began his elaborate stunt by purchasing a one-way ticket from

Seattle to Tacoma on Northwest Airlines flight 305. Although barely half-full, the flight contained more than enough hostages for Cooper's needs. While the aircraft was still on the tarmac at Seattle, he handed a stewardess a note setting out his demands for US$200,000 in unmarked notes, four parachutes and, reportedly, 'no funny stuff'.

Unfortunately, the stewardess mistook the note for a proposition of some kind, and failed to read it until the aircraft was airborne. When she then confronted Cooper, he responded by showing her the contents of his bag, which appeared to resemble a bomb.

At this point, the 727 changed its course and returned to Seattle where the FBI was waiting. Rather than storm the aircraft, it complied with Cooper's demands for the ransom and parachutes, having first taken note of the serial numbers of all 10,000 of the $20 bills. It could not run the risk of tampering with the parachutes as it could not be certain that Cooper would not take hostages with him.

Having received what he had asked for, Cooper then demanded that the aircraft be flown to Mexico. To enable him to make his jump, he insisted on certain conditions being met: the aircraft was to fly with its landing gear and flaps down, in order to slow its progress; its speed was not to exceed 273 km/h (170 mph); and its altitude was to be restricted to 3,048m (10,000 ft).

Complying with these conditions, the pilots realized that they would not be able to reach Mexico without refuelling, and so informed Cooper that they would have to land at Reno. Cooper agreed to this without complaint. In hindsight, it appears that he had never intended to go to Mexico after all.

The aircraft then departed for Reno, but shortly after take-off the crew, who had been confined to the front cabin away from Cooper, noticed the flashing of a warning indicator light, showing that Cooper had opened the rear hatch. About ten minutes later, at 8.11pm, the crew felt pressure bumps, suggesting that Cooper had made his jump. He was never seen again.

It seemed that Cooper was not only an extraordinary escape artist, but that he was also blessed with exceptional powers of endurance, since the conditions into which he had jumped were abominable. Wearing only a suit, shoes and a parachute, he had leapt from a considerable height directly into a snowstorm. The temperature at 3,048m was estimated to be -22°C outside the aircraft, with a wind chill factor of -57°C.

Even if he had survived such a descent (which is possible as it would have taken less than a minute), Cooper still had to land safely in a forest in complete darkness and then find his way out without dying of exposure or being caught by the authorities.

The FBI launched a huge operation, using every available resource, to try to find Cooper. They calculated the search area by assessing information from the flight crew, which gave them a rough idea of where he might have landed. Attempts were also made to pursue the aircraft in both fixed-wing aircraft and helicopters and a massive search on the ground was mounted. No evidence of Cooper was ever found, and the FBI remained baffled by his escape.

The mystery was to deepen almost a decade later, on the other side of the country. In February 1980 in Vancouver, Washington, a boy named Brian Ingram uncovered a portion of the money while digging a hole in a riverbank. The notes were not in good condition, but it was possible to discern the serial numbers, which matched some of those used in the ransom payment. However, the location and quantity of notes found simply created further confusion among the authorities. As well as being a great distance away from the area where Cooper had jumped, Ingram had discovered only US$5,800 of the original US$200,000.

Even though this find suggests that Cooper, or at least part of the ransom, survived, really all that the world is left with is a series of questions. Where is Cooper now? Where is the remaining US$194,200? Was the money buried in Washington to act as a decoy? Did Cooper fool everyone by jumping at a different moment to what was thought, and in so doing ruin the FBI's calculations? Did he have an accomplice waiting for him? Whatever the answers, Cooper's daring feat remains one of the most perplexing and infamous unsolved crimes to this day.

AMELIA EARHART

Amelia Earhart was a pioneer, both in terms of aviation and in the advancement of women's rights. Not only was she one of the first women to be issued with a pilot's licence by the FAI (Federation Aeronautique Internationale) in America in 1923, but she also went on to break several aviation records in the years that followed, earning herself a prodigious reputation. No wonder, then, that her failure to return from a record-breaking attempt in 1937 was the most high-profile disappearance of the time, and remains as much a mystery today as it was then.

One of Earhart's greatest accomplishments took place in 1932, when she became the first woman to fly across the Atlantic. In doing so, she also set a new record of 13 hours and 30 minutes of continuous flying, despite the fact that the journey had almost ended in tragedy on more than one occasion, with Earhart being beset by several major setbacks. The first of these was a serious lightning storm that almost caused her to crash into the Atlantic. Then, as she approached the coast of Europe, she realized that her aircraft was leaking fuel and she was forced to make an emergency landing in a field in Ireland. In spite of these challenges, Earhart successfully completed the flight and her name entered the history books.

Having crossed the Atlantic, Earhart decided to go one step further. In 1935 she flew across the Pacific from Hawaii to California. This feat also ended in triumph and, her confidence boosted, Earhart began to plan an airborne circumnavigation of the globe at its widest point – the Equator. The trip was too difficult and perilous for anyone, even Earhart, to attempt alone, so she asked Fred Noonan to accompany her as a navigator.

Earhart and Noonan were last seen when they took off from Lae, New Guinea, on the most treacherous leg of the flight. At this point they were just two days and around 11,000km (6,835 miles) away from completing the courageous journey. Their destination was a tiny piece of land in the Pacific known as Howland Island.

Although the weather conditions had been good when the pair left Lae, the sky rapidly became overcast, disrupting navigation. However, Earhart

Amelia Earhart poses for the press corps beside her plane.

and Noonan still had support, in the form of radio contact with the Coast Guard cutter *Itasca*. Then, at 7.42am on 2 July 1937, the *Itasca* received a message from Earhart stating: 'cannot see you, gas is running low, been unable to reach you by radio, we are flying at 1,000 feet [sic]... one half-hour fuel and no landfall'.

The *Itasca* responded by creating a beacon of thick black smoke and ordering all ships in the area to switch on every light available to assist the stricken aircraft. Earhart managed to make one final contact with the ship, in which she gave her assumed position. This was effectively the last that was ever heard of her.

In an effort to try to locate Earhart and Noonan, the USA launched the largest search and rescue operation that had ever been attempted. Unfortunately, in spite of combing vast areas of ocean, the search teams failed to locate the pair, and abandoned their quest.

The flyers were reported as missing, presumed dead, and the world could only guess at what had happened to them. To add to the mystery, sightings of the famous pair were made long after the search had been concluded. In his 1987 book, *Eyewitness: the Amelia Earhart Incident*, Thomas E. Devine (a former American GI) claimed that the pair had been spotted alive and well on the Japanese-held island of Saipan during the Second World War. Following the publication of this book, several other GIs came forward to corroborate the story, lending it some credence.

However, when Saipan was invaded by the US in 1944, no trace of the pilot and her navigator was ever found. All that is known for sure is that Amelia Earhart and Fred Noonan vanished somewhere over the Pacific Ocean on 2 July 1937. No one can be certain how two such experienced flyers could disappear under such circumstances, or why their radio seemed to fail at such a crucial moment. Unless further evidence comes to light, these questions will remain unanswered and people will continue to speculate over what really happened to these two courageous aviators.

GLENN MILLER

Glenn Miller not only enjoyed great acclaim as a musician and entertainer, but also served as an officer in the US Air Force during the Second World War. His successful combination of the two roles earned him great respect and he played a large part in boosting the morale of the Allied troops during the conflict.

So it was a huge shock to the world when, having boarded an aircraft in England on 15 December 1944, he disappeared into oblivion. He had been on his way to Paris to conclude arrangements with his band for the Christmas Day concert for Allied troops, but he never reached his destination. The true reason for his disappearance remains unknown to this day, although there has been much speculation as to what happened to the famous performer.

It was not unusual during the 1930s and 1940s for aircraft to vanish inexplicably. Such losses were not confined to the Bermuda Triangle but occurred all over the world. While no one could be sure of the reasons for these disappearances, the most probable explanation was that it was mechanical failure because of the fledgling nature of the aviation industry at that time.

Aside from this possibility, two main theories (one from each opposing side of the war) have been put forward to explain what happened to Miller. The German tabloid newspaper *Bild* claimed that Miller had died from a cardiac arrest while in the company of a prostitute. It was suggested that these facts had been covered up by the British and Americans in order to protect the troops' morale. No evidence has ever come to light to support this claim and the Allies dismissed it as mere propaganda.

The Allies maintained that Miller's light aircraft, a Norseman UC-64, had encountered bad weather which had caused it to ditch in the English Channel. It is certainly true that Miller's flight had been delayed for several days by stormy conditions, so there might be some truth behind this theory.

Recently, however, fresh evidence has come to light that may suggest a completely different explanation and might, indeed, reveal elements of

Glenn Miller photographed for a band publicity shot before the US entered the Second World War.

a cover-up on the part of the Allies. This new information is contained in the logbook of an RAF navigator, Fred Shaw, and may hold the key to the disappearance. In fact, the revelations within its pages have been described by the Ministry of Defence as 'the most likely solution to the mystery'.

During the war, Shaw carried out bombing raids in an Avro Lancaster, and his records show that, on the day in question, his bomber had been recalled from a raid over Germany due to bad weather. It was usual in these cases for bombers to jettison their load over the sea as a precaution before landing. For this purpose there were specially marked jettison areas which all aircraft were advised to avoid.

It is entirely possible that either Miller's aircraft strayed into this no-go zone, or else the bomber dropped its load outside the defined boundaries. Whatever the case, the bomber reported seeing a small aircraft hit the water after being thrown off track by the bombs.

Whether or not these facts were known to the Allied command at the time is another mystery in itself. It is unlikely, however, that they would have run the risk of damaging public morale during the war. Sixty years later, the truth of the matter may finally be coming to light.

FLIGHT 19

One of the most intriguing disappearances of all time was the loss of an entire squadron of aircraft, which vanished without trace, leaving no clue as to what had happened. The occurrence engendered much controversy, not only because there were conflicting views on the exact circumstances behind the event, but also because it kick-started the mythical reputation surrounding the area of the disappearance, the now infamous Bermuda Triangle in the Atlantic Ocean.

All kinds of explanations have been put forward in an attempt to understand the puzzle. Some blame freak weather conditions, whilst others, more bizarrely, believe that the squadron may even have been kidnapped by aliens. This theory was popularized by Stephen Spielberg in his film *Close Encounters of the Third Kind*, in which the pilots of Flight 19 were shown being returned to Earth in an alien spacecraft.

This intriguing case poses many questions. How was it possible that not one, but all five planes in a squadron, with several experts on board, could vanish so inexplicably? Even more bewildering was the fact that the search and rescue plane that was sent after them was also lost, for reasons that are still unknown.

Flight 19 – consisting of five Naval Avenger torpedo-bombers –

departed Fort Lauderdale on a training flight on 5 December 1945. Each of the five planes was supposed to have had three men on board, but on the day in question, one had failed to appear, so that this flight consisted of 14 airmen in total. Of these, 13 were in the final stages of their training, although all of them were more than capable of handling their aircraft. The exercise was being led by Lt Charles Taylor, a highly experienced pilot, who had acquired much expertise in flying over the Florida Keys.

Their flight plan was to conduct a practice bombing run over an area known as the 'Hen and Chickens Shoals' that lay to the east of the Florida Keys. The squadron was then to continue to fly east over the ocean until it was around 190km (118 miles) from the shore, before turning north for another 113km (70 miles). It would then turn south-west and return to base. This triangular course would take the aircraft over the Bahamas, and would steer them almost continuously through the Bermuda Triangle.

The flight took off at 2.10pm in good weather, although conditions looked as if they might take a marked turn for the worse towards the evening. After less than two hours, just before 4.00pm, Fort Lauderdale received a radio transmission in which Lt Taylor stated that the squadron's compasses were not working and the pilots believed themselves to be lost. It is now known that the Bermuda Triangle is one of two areas of the world – the other being the Devil's Triangle in Asia – in which there is an unusual level of magnetic interference which can adversely affect compass readings. Could this be the reason behind the loss of so many ships and aircraft in the region?

Lt Taylor reported over the radio that he believed that the squadron was flying over the Florida Keys. He was advised that, if he was certain of this, he should direct the aircraft north towards Miami and the mainland.

If, as is thought today, Lt Taylor was mistaken and he was in fact over the Bahamas, then by flying north, Flight 19 would have taken itself further out into the Atlantic Ocean and away from safety.

No one had any reason to suspect that this was the case, however, and the squadron continued northwards. To complicate matters further, atmospheric interference from the approaching storm, coupled with the radio waves from commercial radio broadcasts in nearby Cuba, were hampering efforts to communicate with the flight. Taylor was urged to switch to the emergency frequency, which would have facilitated radio communication, but he refused. One of the aircraft was encountering problems with its radio, and Taylor feared that by changing frequencies he might lose contact with it altogether.

As time passed, the sense of urgency at the Fort Lauderdale base increased. As it was winter, the sun was due to set at around 5.30pm, and bad weather conditions were moving down from the north.

At 5.15pm, radio contact was briefly re-established, and Taylor informed the base that the flight was now heading west. He was heard advising the squadron to remain close together. The plan was that when the first aircraft ran out of fuel the remaining bombers would all ditch in the sea, thus increasing the likelihood of everyone surviving.

A Dumb seaplane, the first of several rescue aircraft, was launched shortly after 6.00pm, but rapidly lost contact with the shore. This was attributed to the bad weather, which had caused an antenna to become iced-over. Nevertheless, it seemed that the base had lost another of its machines. A further aircraft, a Martin Mariner, was then sent after the seaplane, but, once more, radio contact was lost. Whether this was again due to the weather is unknown, but shortly after the Mariner had failed to appear at the scheduled rendezvous, the crew of a nearby ship reported sighting an aircraft that exploded. They were unable to attempt any kind of rescue as by now the conditions at sea were atrocious.

What is so baffling about this disappearance is that no survivors, bodies or debris from the lost squadron were ever found. Although the poor weather may have had a large role to play, no one could be sure of exactly what had happened, and a US Navy inquest attributed the disaster to 'causes or reasons unknown'. To this day, it is a complete mystery how an entire squadron of aircraft could simply disappear when it was so close to its home coastline.

USS *CYCLOPS*

In its day, the USS *Cyclops* was the largest ship to serve as a collier in the US Navy's fleet, and it was capable of carrying more than 10,000 tons of cargo and in excess of 300 seamen. It seems incredible, therefore, that in March 1918 it sailed into the Bermuda Triangle and disappeared without a trace, with the loss of all hands. No distress signal was issued and the US Navy was unable to understand what had happened.

The *Cyclops* was commissioned for military service on 1 May 1917, upon America's entry into the First World War. In 1918 the vessel was assigned to the Naval Overseas Transportation Service, where its main role was to refuel the British ships that were patrolling the South Atlantic, specifically the waters around Brazil. On 4 March, the *Cyclops* set sail from Barbados, bound for Norfolk, Virginia. What was to be its last complete voyage would take the ship directly through the infamous waters of the Bermuda Triangle.

When the vessel disappeared, it was originally thought that it had been torpedoed, but a search of German records after the war discounted this theory, as did the fact that no wreckage was ever found. The latter factor also made it unlikely that the ship had struck a mine. In either event, surely at least some of the crew would have been able to escape by lifeboat?

More recent attempts at explaining the tragedy have turned to the mysterious nature of the Bermuda Triangle itself. There are a number of conditions found in this area that make it a particularly treacherous place for both ships and aircraft.

Firstly, it is one of two places on Earth where compasses do not point towards true north. This can result in massive navigational errors that could spell disaster for a heavily laden vessel such as the *Cyclops*.

To accompany this ever-present hazard are the erratic and turbulent weather patterns of the Caribbean Atlantic, which is frequently ravaged by anything from water spouts to storms and hurricanes. As if this were not enough, the currents are rapid and strong, and can not only alter the location of sandbanks, but can also drag ships on to reefs.

A picture of USS Cyclops, *taken shortly before she mysteriously disappeared in 1918.*

Another lesser-known – yet equally deadly – factor could also have caused the disappearance of the *Cyclops*. There are recorded cases of the spontaneous venting of large quantities of natural gas located under the sea, as a result of a huge build-up of pressure. This natural phenomenon can change the density of the seawater, causing any nearby vessel to sink in an instant. Without further proof, however, it is difficult to be sure whether this was the reason behind the disappearance of the *Cyclops*.

In a further strange twist, the *Cyclops'* three sister ships – the *Nereus*, the *Proteus* and the *Jupiter* – all met with unhappy endings. The *Nereus* and *Proteus* both served as colliers in the Second World War and were sunk by U-boats in the Atlantic, with the loss of all hands. The *Jupiter*, re-named the *Langley* and converted into the US Navy's first aircraft-carrier, was sunk by the Japanese off the coast of Java in 1942. Chillingly, all four members of this nautical family now lie somewhere at the bottom of the ocean, having claimed more than 1,000 lives among them.

What really happened in the case of the *Cyclops* is almost impossible to determine due to the lack of evidence of any sort. As it is not known exactly where the ship went down, it is almost impossible to hunt for a wreck, and until such time as any telltale scraps of wreckage are found, there will only ever be theories. Thus the tragic fate of the *Cyclops*, the largest US Navy vessel ever to have disappeared inexplicably, remains a mystery.

THE LOST TREASURE OF THE AZTECS

The legend of the wealth of the Aztecs has been in existence ever since civilization was found on the continent. The original Spaniards who set sail from Cuba to explore the coast of Mexico had the pursuit of riches firmly fixed in their minds. When the first of these Spanish explorers returned to Cuba with finely worked gold, it did not take long for them to return in greater numbers to investigate further.

It is hard to tell whether the great trove of treasure actually existed, or whether it was simply a product of the different values of the two colliding cultures. The Meso-Americans valued gold for its beauty and did not revere it in the same way as the European invaders. Gold ornaments were worn freely by the native people, who appeared to prize it no more highly than items such as beautiful feathers.

When the Spanish arrived in Mexico with finely crafted glass beads, the inhabitants were only too glad to trade their gold for these strange new objects of beauty as they had an entirely different monetary value system. When the Spanish saw the native people handing over their gold with such ease, they began to believe that in this land gold must be incredibly abundant for it to be distributed so freely.

To a certain extent the Europeans were right – at that time the untapped mineral wealth of the country was very great, as they quickly realized when they began to mine the resources of the Americas. The ease with which they acquired the gold from the Aztecs must have fired both their imaginations and their greed. As a result, it did not take long for the legend of Eldorado, the city of gold, to take shape and develop.

When Moctezuma, the king of the Aztecs, realized that the invaders were eager to acquire gold, he bestowed lavish gifts upon them, hoping to satisfy their needs. The giving of gifts was a polite ritual for the Aztecs, and the Spaniards in turn gave gifts of cloth and beads, which were, in truth, of little value to them. As the Spaniards pushed ever further inland towards his city in an insatiable quest for more gold, the Aztec king grew increasingly desperate, almost emptying the royal coffers in order to please the Spanish.

The Spaniards misinterpreted this generosity as a sign of even greater wealth. Surely, they thought, if the king could afford to give away such valuable gifts, he must have vaults absolutely brimming with gold. The invaders sent much of this gold back to Spain, as a gift to their own king and as a bid for more support, fully expecting to discover more riches when they conquered the city of Tenochtitlan.

On this point, however, the Conquistadors were sorely mistaken. When they took command of the city, they found that the hoard of gold was much smaller than expected. On discovering this, they demanded that all citizens hand over every item of gold they possessed. Once this had been amassed, the Conquistadors were more satisfied, but it was around now that events began to turn against them.

Angry at being invaded and plundered, the natives turned against the Spanish. A great battle ensued and the Spanish were driven from Tenochtitlan, over the long causeways crossing the lake that encircled the city. The Spaniards were outnumbered by more than one hundred to one, and although they attempted to carry their hoard of treasure out with them on mules, they were unable to protect it and the majority was lost in the lake. Many men drowned because they were laden down with so much precious metal.

If these stories are true, it is entirely possible that the treasure still exists, somewhere in Mexico, where it has remained hidden for centuries. Only comparatively recently – in the 1980s – was the Templo Major, the central ceremonial pyramid of Tenochtitlan, discovered in the very centre of Mexico City. Workers had been digging a tunnel for a new metro stop when they discovered this architectural treasure. There may be much more than this still waiting to be discovered, buried in the foundations of one of the world's largest cities. The Aztecs may even have buried some of the gold in an effort to hide it from the invaders, either in the city or up in the mountains.

There is also the possibility that the Conquistadors did discover a large amount of gold, but concealed its true quantity in order to avoid handing it over to their king. Alternatively, in their greed, they may have miscalculated and found there was just not as much gold in existence as they had originally believed. There is a very real likelihood that this last explanation has some basis in truth, given the avaricious behaviour of the Spaniards and the lengths they went to in order to secure the gold.

Time passed and the Spaniards had renewed success in their invasion efforts, while they continued to search for further riches. Their conquest extended south into South America, where they continued the orgy of greed and destruction against the Incas. It seems likely that they were spurred on by the stories they had heard about the riches of Mexico.

Although history maintains that the Spaniards never actually found the ultimate hoard of the Aztecs, it remains unclear as to whether this is actually the truth. However much gold they found, it is unlikely that they would ever have been satisfied. What is certain is that Aztec gold did exist, as quantities of it have been recovered today, but whether there is a huge hoard still waiting to be discovered remains shrouded in mystery.

THE DINOSAURS

In the long history of life on Earth, countless species have become extinct. Of these, perhaps the best known and certainly the most intriguing has been the disappearance of the dinosaurs. For millions of years, these huge beasts were the unquestionable masters of the planet, living on every continent of the world with nothing to challenge their supremacy.

However, there came a point, around 65 million years ago, when the reign of one of the most successful life forms ever to exist came to an end. Just why this happened is an enduring mystery, and although a number of theories have been put forward over the years, they have yet to be proven.

The theories are based upon what slim evidence still exists from the period. By examining rock and fossil formations, some vital information can be gleaned about what may have happened in the past. From these studies, experts have established that, at the time of the disappearance of the dinosaurs, there was great upheaval in progress on Earth.

Examination of the natural history of the planet has enabled scientists to draw a line between the age of the dinosaurs and the age of the mammals which followed. This boundary between two different periods of life on Earth separates the older Cretaceous period (the time of the dinosaurs) from the later Tertiary period (the time of the mammals, which we, as humans, inhabit). Geologists refer to the former age as 'K', and to the latter as 'T' – thus the mass disappearance of the dinosaurs has become known as the 'K-T extinctions'. It was not only the dinosaurs that became extinct, however: as much as half of all life on Earth ceased.

Geologists have established that the huge disturbances that occurred on the planet were climatic in nature. It seems that conditions altered dramatically and Earth ceased to be the relatively temperate and stable planet that it had been throughout the Mesozoic era. Instead, it became the cooler and more changeable world that we know today and, as time went on, a number of ice ages occurred. The speed at which these changes took place at the time of the K-T boundary is a source of great mystery. What could have caused such a rapid change?

Two main theories have been put forward to explain what happened. Some people believe that the change was as a result of a gradual process originating from the activity of the Earth itself. Others are of the opinion that there was some kind of massive cataclysmic event, such as a meteor strike on the planet. Both arguments have a substantial amount of evidence to support them.

Those who support the idea of a more gradual climate change believe that it may have been caused by sustained massive volcanic eruptions over a long period of time. This would have caused a 'greenhouse' effect and altered the global climate dramatically. This theory is lent credence by the fact that geologists are certain that there was indeed a time of increased volcanic activity towards the end of the Cretaceous period.

However, just as there is convincing evidence for the idea of volcanic activity, there is also a very plausible argument to support the notion of a meteor impact. Indeed, it is even possible that perhaps both took place. Researchers discovered iridium dust, trapped in the layers of rock that correspond to the time of around 65 million years ago. This unusual substance was present in sufficient quantities to indicate that it could only have come from one of two places. Either it had originated from space, in which case the dust could have been released into the atmosphere as a result of a meteor impact, or its source was the molten mantle of the Earth which is comparatively rich in iridium.

In addition to looking within Earth's structure, scientists have also examined its external appearance, in an effort to try to understand what happened. One of the major problems they have faced, however, is that the planet looks radically different today from how it would have appeared 65 million years ago. This makes it extremely difficult to locate any evidence of either volcanic eruptions or a meteor crater. In 1980, however, a discovery was made that was thought to provide the proof that scientists were looking for.

It seems that a large portion of the Gulf of Mexico is actually an enormous crater. Known as the Chicxulub Crater, it forms the edge of part of the Yucatan Peninsular. The rock formations in the area contain large amounts of shocked quartz, which is formed by violent tremors such as those that occur as a result of an impact. It was estimated that, in order to create such a crater, the meteor would have had to be at least 10km (6.2 miles) in diameter. A collision of this magnitude is large enough to have had a truly global effect.

If such a meteor had hit Earth, enormous volcanic eruptions would have thrown large amounts of soot into the air and released noxious gases. These would have caused acid rain, which would have poisoned the water supply and destroyed plant life. The quantity of particles in the atmosphere would also have led to a cooling of the Earth, as less sunlight would have been able to penetrate the atmosphere. The effect of this would have been similar to that of a nuclear winter.

Bearing in mind that dinosaurs are believed to have been cold-blooded animals, the effect of this global cooling would have been catastrophic. Many animals would have been reduced to torpor, as their metabolisms would have slowed down due to the extreme cold. Food supplies would also have dwindled, as disruptions at the lower end of the food chain, caused by the loss of plant life, affected the carnivores at the upper end. Most must have died of malnutrition.

As time progressed, the climate would have been dragged in the opposite direction. After the initial cooling down of the Earth, the increased number of greenhouse gases would have caused it gradually to warm up again – eventually becoming even warmer than it had been originally. Most creatures can only live within certain set parameters of temperature, and those with the capacity to survive the original cooling may then have expired when the subsequent warming took place.

Such extremes would have had a less notable effect on small mammalian creatures since their warm blood would have given them greater protection against these sharp changes. Thus it is to these mammals that some people look in order to explain the demise of the dinosaurs.

One theory is that the survival of the mammals was not merely a question of them out-evolving the dinosaurs but also of them being better adapted to survive the changing environment.

After all, it seems that the dinosaurs had reached a new peak of their evolutionary scale shortly before they became extinct, with giant carnivores such as Tyrannosaurus Rex evolving relatively shortly before the end. Rather, it has been postulated that the mammals simply ate all of the dinosaurs' eggs and thus reduced their numbers. However, this is an extremely difficult hypothesis to prove either way.

The focus upon the eggs is interesting for another reason. Many modern reptile eggs are very sensitive to changes in temperature while they are incubating and any fluctuations can affect the sex of the creature when it hatches. A sustained period of climate change could have led to a huge imbalance in the numbers of males and females, and so had a disastrous effect on their breeding potential and survival rates.

Although the dinosaurs are the most highly publicized species to have suddenly become extinct, they are certainly not the only ones. To date, science has recorded five mass extinctions on Earth, of which the end of the dinosaurs was by no means the worst. At the end of the Permian era (290–248 million years ago), for example, more than 90 per cent of all life on the planet was wiped out. Why?

Some scientists have stipulated that there is an element of regularity in these extinctions and that, aside from the asteroid impact theory, there may be another cosmic cause. Perhaps there is a comet or cloud of debris in space that only comes into contact with Earth every 25 million years or so. To date, this idea remains to be proven and generally receives far less support than the other theories examined so far.

The science involved in determining the causes of mass extinctions is of great relevance to us today. Human beings have become arguably the most potent force to act upon the world and we have a degree of ability to shape and control our environment. However, this sense of power can be deceptive and we should be prepared to expect the unexpected.

The dinosaurs, too, were the dominant species and yet their reign was brought to an abrupt end. Whether this was due to a single event such as a meteor, or as a result of a slower process of volcanic and tectonic activity, we cannot be certain. It could just as easily have been a combination of the two factors, or it could even have been caused by another factor altogether that has not survived, such as a plague or parasite.

An unforeseen cataclysmic event, such as a meteor strike, could potentially annihilate our planet and, for all our presumed power, we are just as vulnerable as the dinosaurs. This fear has been reflected in the large amount of popular entertainment which depicts huge apocalyptic disasters befalling the planet, with mankind being powerless to resist, despite all its scientific advances.

Only now is it genuinely being considered that such a horror, in the form of global climate change, may actually be caused by mankind itself.

Perhaps we, as human beings, should look at the fate of the dinosaurs and take heed. Many people believe that the rapid progression of technology in the last century or so may be causing the drastic changes in our weather patterns which have been notable for both their frequency and ferocity. The fact that the dinosaurs were most likely killed by such climate change should give us food for thought and send a shiver down our spines.

The changes to our present climate are believed to be responsible for a rate of species extinction that is easily comparable to any of the great mass extinctions of the past. This alarming information has led many scientists to believe that we may potentially be teetering on the threshold of another such extinction.

This can only give us greater impetus to understand the reason why the dinosaurs disappeared. By unravelling the mystery of their extinction, perhaps we will stand a better chance of preventing our own.

LOST WORLDS

The existence of civilizations and our awareness of them have not always been synchronized, a factor which has distorted our view of history and our perception of the capabilities of earlier people. Throughout the history of mankind, cities and states have sprung up all over the world, achieved their age of greatness and then subsided back into the dust from which they came.

Some of these lost worlds leave written evidence of their great achievements encrypted in a forgotten language, such as the Egyptian hieroglyph or the Mayan codex. Others may leave behind little more than a puzzling legacy of monuments or even just the legends of their existence.

THE DOGON

The people of the Dogon tribe, in Mali, West Africa, live in small villages miles from anywhere. The nearest civilization is the remote city of Timbuktu. Despite their apparent geographical and cultural isolation, this remote tribe have been in possession of astronomical knowledge that, although now overtaken, was for hundreds of years far in advance of Western understanding.

The first Western scientists to make contact with the Dogon were a pair of French anthropologists – Dr Marcel Griale and Dr Germaine Dieterien – who reached the tribe in 1931. Astonished by what they found there, they remained in Mali to research this people for more than 30 years. During this time, they gained access to the Dogon's religious and cultural traditions, and eventually came to earn their trust.

The secret tribal lore of the Dogon revealed that they possessed some fascinating information. Long before Galileo made his revolutionary discoveries in Europe, the Dogon seem to have had knowledge of the rings of Saturn. They were also aware of the existence of the four major moons of Jupiter and knew that the Earth is a planet, and that all planets orbit the sun.

The tribe also had an extensive understanding of the Sirius binary star system, which was unknown to the West until 1862, when it was spotted from the world's most powerful telescope. The Dogon were fully aware that Sirius actually comprises two stars, Sirius A and Sirius B, which orbit each other in a 50-year cycle with the result that, for a large part of this cycle, only one of the two stars is ever visible.

Sirius A – a bright star that we refer to as the Dog Star – was to the Dogon the most important star in the sky, as they believed that it was here that life originated. Sirius B – which we have discovered is 100,000 times less visible than its twin, and which we class as a 'White Dwarf' star – was known to the Dogon as the second star of this system and described by them as 'the heaviest star'.

Such ideas are relatively recent in modern astronomy yet the Dogon

A Dogon tribesman with his daughter in southern Mali.

were aware of this information long before instruments such as telescopes were invented. The mystery deepens still further when we consider the tribe's own explanation of how they acquired their detailed astronomical knowledge. According to tribal lore, they were given this information by a race of god-like extra-terrestrials, the Nommo, who originated from the Sirius star system.

Dogon legend tells how the Nommo arrived on a type of spaceship, accompanied by fire and thunder. These aliens were terrifying in their appearance, being fish-like and bearing similarities to the amphibious gods of some other ancient religions such as the Egyptian Isis and the Babylonian Oannes. According to tribal lore, these aquatic beings released huge quantities of water on to the Earth in which to live.

The Dogon referred to Sirius B as 'the Nommo star', and also spoke of a mystical third star, Sirius C, which, to date, has not been recognized by modern science. The tribe called this star the 'Sun of Women', and predicted that it would re-appear in the sky when the Nommo choose to reveal themselves to Earth once again.

The Dogon, therefore, have their own explanation as to how they acquired their remarkable knowledge. But what does the wider world think? Three main theories have been put forward to explain the mystery, and all have their proponents and detractors.

Firstly, it has been suggested that the Dogon may have learned about Sirius through an undocumented contact with the outside world. However, this argument would seem to be invalidated by the fact that the tribe's knowledge of Sirius was documented on cuneiform tablets many years before modern science even became aware of the star system.

Secondly, it is possible that one of the great ancient civilizations, such as Egypt or Persia, was itself in possession of this astronomical knowledge and had passed it on to a member of the Dogon, perhaps a wandering tribal nomad. This theory seems unlikely, however, since by nature the Dogon people choose to live a life of isolation away from the rest of the world.

The third possible explanation is that perhaps an ancient visionary priest or psychic prophesied this information to the tribe and it became woven into Dogon mythology. However, this seems almost as remarkable an idea as the tribe's own explanation. It seems that perhaps it is the Dogon's own account that we should, after all, take as being the correct one. After all, these people have been proved right on numerous counts already. The fact of their isolation and ignorance of the Western world's wider theories pertaining to alien beings lends their explanation further credence. How else could they give a description of an extra-terrestrial unless they had actually encountered one?

The mystery remains, but what seems likely is that supposedly 'primitive' tribes such as the Dogon were, in fact, a lot more advanced than was thought possible.

CIUDAD BLANCA

Hidden somewhere in the vast, impenetrable jungle of the Central American coast is the legendary 'Ciudad Blanca', or 'White City'. The city is said to have contained incredible wealth and yet was abandoned hundreds of years ago for unknown reasons. Although a number of international expeditions have endeavoured to uncover its secret location and sophisticated satellite technology has been used, the density of the jungle spanning Nicaragua and Honduras is so great that, to date, the task has been impossible.

The first recorded mention of the 'Ciudad Blanca' dates back to 1526, when it was referred to by Hernando Cortes – the Spanish conqueror of Mexico – by the twin names of Xucutaco and Hueitapalan. It is unsurprising that the Spanish were interested in the city as it was said that its riches rivalled those of Tenochtitlan, the wealthy Aztec capital. Inspired by such a notion, Cortes sent many of his followers in search of the lost kingdom, but the treacherous nature of the Mosquito Coast prevented the Conquistadors from finding it and they soon abandoned their search.

It is thought, however, that, even by the time of the Conquistadors, the 'Ciudad Blanca' was in decline. At that time the area was inhabited by the Pech people, who are believed to have originated from South America. Many skirmishes are recorded as having taken place between the Pech and the Spanish, as well as with the neighbouring tribes.

So what happened to this city, and how did it come to be abandoned? One possible theory is that it may just have exceeded its natural limits of expansion and was thus abandoned. Or perhaps, already shrinking, it was ultimately unable to survive the arrival of the Conquistadors on the continent, since the Spanish invaders altered the balance of an entire way of life and had a damaging effect on many of the formerly advanced and prosperous civilizations of Meso-America.

The speed at which the jungle of the Mosquito Coast could devour an empty city is remarkable, especially as, prior to the arrival of the Spanish, it had been an incredibly populous area of the world. The 'Ciudad Blanca' is only one of the many undiscovered cities that are hidden in Central

America, but for modern Honduras it will be a national and cultural treasure should it ever be recovered.

THE ANASAZI

Little known today, the Anasazi civilization existed for almost 1,000 years in the area of the USA now called Arizona and New Mexico. At their cultural peak, in around AD1050, the Anasazi were a thriving community, who built huge structures in which to live. Palaces, some containing up to 500 rooms, were cut into the cliffs and many displayed a considerable complexity of construction. However, by the middle of the 12th century, the society had collapsed and its population had scattered. By AD1300 the tribe had disappeared altogether. The reasons why are unknown to this day.

Early explorers and relic collectors were amazed by what they found of this tribe, uncovering a remarkable abundance of abandoned pottery and artefacts. Initially, the discoveries were credited to the distant Aztecs as it was believed that the indigenous people living in this region would be incapable of constructing such an organised community. Only later did it become apparent that another civilization altogether may have been responsible.

The greatest development of structures built by the Anasazi was discovered at Chaco Canyon, New Mexico, and was believed to have been the hub of a community of outlying farms and settlements. Several huge palaces were located here and it is thought that trading, spiritual ceremonies and astronomy were all practised in this central area. Is it conceivable that such a sophisticated community could just vanish?

It has not been unknown over the course of history for civilizations to decline or disappear. Some peoples – such as the residents of Pompeii or the Minoans of Crete – are known to have been wiped out as a result of natural disaster, but the fate of other civilizations remains a cause for speculation. What we do know is that there are numerous factors that could bring about the demise of a civilized society, such as drought, famine or war. At some sites, such as those where burned dwellings have been found, the sad fate of the inhabitants is all too apparent.

The rise and fall of some cities or states has been well documented over time, giving us the opportunity to learn from the mistakes and misfortunes of the past. It is true to say that, at any time, our hold on the status quo is only ever a precarious one, and if we can avoid repeating some of the errors made by our forebears, perhaps we can really be said to have made progress.

THE MAYA AND THE AZTEC

The Mayan and Aztec civilizations are both fascinating examples of advanced cultures in Central America, developed long before the arrival of the Spanish invaders. Although the Mayans preceded the Aztecs, the two peoples shared a number of common belief systems, particularly in matters such as astronomy, religion and ritual sacrifice, and both built large observatories, temples and pyramids in which to conduct these practices.

The Mayan culture reached its height between AD900 and AD1200. During this period their influence spread across a huge area of Central America and they were trading with nations as far away as Peru. One of their strengths was the quality of their architecture and construction, which was so advanced that, even today, there are examples of buried temples and pyramids to be found all over the Yucatan Peninsula of Mexico.

Concepts of space and time were extraordinarily significant to the Maya. They used a highly complex system to mark the passage of time, establishing a calendar that gave each day its own specific name, in line with precise astronomical calculations. As the cycle progressed, any cosmic event, such as a planetary transit, was treated with great reverence.

Central to the Mayan religious and cosmic beliefs was ritual human sacrifice. Such bloodshed was deemed to be particularly necessary at the time of the solar eclipse, in order to meet the needs of the gods.

When a full revolution had been made through the possible sequences of calendar days, the system would then start again, giving an inbuilt cycle of rebirth and regeneration. Each time this happened, great events were predicted to take place. Interestingly, this is expected to happen again soon, giving the modern world an opportunity to assess the accuracy of Mayan prophecy.

It is believed that conditions such as drought or disease, together with warfare, drove the Maya into decline and by AD1300 they were building constructions that were of markedly inferior quality. By the time of the Spanish conquest of Mexico in the early 1500s, many of the great ruins of the Maya that one can visit today in Mexico were already lost or abandoned.

As the Mayan civilization collapsed, a number of other cultures in the region were in the ascendant, most notable of which were the Aztecs. When the Spaniards first came into contact with these people, they were astonished by what they saw. Large indigenous populations lived in elegant cities based around vast pyramids and ceremonial centres. The riches and splendour of the ruling class seemed incomparable, and they were amazed at the high standard of social development. Yet the Spanish were shocked when they discovered the huge extent of ritual human sacrifice being performed in these temples and pyramids.

The Aztecs practised the same form of sacrifice as the Maya, although perhaps with even greater fervour. Their sacrificial victims would be the captured warriors of opposing tribes, or slaves taken from subject peoples. Slaughter was often performed on a huge scale in order to sanctify newly built temples, consecrated in honour of the gods – excavations of the larger Mexican pyramids have revealed the existence of hundreds of kneeling skeletons buried deep within the foundations. Images of skulls and skeletons would appear on the architecture of the buildings that were constructed specifically for the purposes of human sacrifice.

Some of the rituals almost defy understanding. Some victims faced having their beating hearts cut out with a stone blade by the high priests. The hearts would then be placed on a special altar as an offering, while corpses were cast down the steps of the pyramid and sometimes cannibalized.

Other rituals, performed at a significant turning point in the astral calendar, would involve the flaying of victims' skin from their bodies while they were still alive. A priest would then take the skin and wear it for an entire month. This type of ritual symbolized rebirth, the loss of human skin being akin to the process of renewal inherent in the shedding of the skin of the serpent, a creature revered by the Aztecs.

Over time, this people's appetite for blood increased, and later temples are generally found to have larger quantities of human remains lying beneath them. It seems that once the cycle of bloodshed had begun, it could only get greater and that demands for sacrifice grew in line with the Aztecs' prosperity. One particularly gruesome tale is that recorded by the Spanish Conquistadors, which states that on their arrival in the Aztec capital of Tenochtitlan – the centre of what is now Mexico City – they observed a monument constructed entirely of human skulls. A rough estimate deemed that this structure comprised 125,000 skulls, arranged in a precise geometrical pattern.

This mystical fascination with death seems cruel and alien to us today, yet it was an integral part of the culture of these ancient civilizations, where ways of life had developed over several thousand years in isolation from what was thought of as the 'known world'. The destruction of the Aztecs, although an incredible military feat by Cortes, the leader of the Conquistadors, was ultimately the annihilation of a highly developed culture.

It seems strange that the Conquistadors were initially granted so much leeway on their arrival in Mexico since the Aztec king, Moctezuma, was quite capable of defeating the invaders. In fact, his restraint was due to an ancient prediction which spoke of the future arrival in the land of the god Quetzalcoatl, who would then use his great power and wisdom to help the Aztec and Mexican peoples to achieve greater glory. Also known as the 'feathered serpent', this most revered of beings was described in terms that matched the armoured and bearded newcomers who then arrived from the East – the direction of the rising sun.

Although this prophecy appears to be accurate regarding the arrival of the Spanish, the result was, of course, quite the reverse of what had been predicted. With the arrival of the Spanish invaders, the Aztec culture was destroyed forever, as the Conquistadors saw it as their duty to eliminate every trace of this once mighty people. Thus another of the world's ancient cultures had disappeared forever.

THE MOCHE

The Moche people formed the first great civilization of Peru, preceding both the Chimu and the Incas. Although it is known that the Moche lived for about 1,000 years – from around AD10 until about AD900 – their origins are uncertain. Were they indigenous South American people, or was there any truth in local legends that spoke of the tribe arriving by raft, under the leadership of a heroic figure known as 'Naymlpa'?

Equally mysterious is why the Moche culture ultimately faded from the continent. One theory is that it might have been as a result of war, as surviving cultural treasures, such as art and pottery, dating from the latter part of their era seem to reflect a growing preoccupation with militarism.

The Moche were a particularly progressive people for their time, especially in the fields of architecture and engineering. Their vast and durable buildings – some of which are still standing today – were constructed out of adobe bricks, which were made from mud and then baked in the sun. Amazingly, some of these buildings are estimated to contain as many as 100 million bricks.

One of their notable achievements was the building of Chan Chan, the largest pre-Columbian city in America, and this, like all their cities, served a largely religious function. Most of the buildings and pyramids were used for the purposes of worship and astronomy. Two of the largest surviving pyramids are known as 'Huacas del Sol y de la Luna', or 'Temples of the Sun and the Moon'. The Moche were not the only ancient culture to display a religious preoccupation with the stars, as many of these early civilizations found great meaning in the motion of the heavens.

Another sign of the Moche's sophistication can be found in their unparalleled systems of irrigation, which are used to this day by local farmers. The Moche created hundreds of miles of irrigation channels and canals, which were filled with water purely by the force of gravity. This system allowed them to gather water from high in the Andes and increase their crop yields. At the height of their success, the region was more highly cultivated and productive than it is today.

Unfortunately, the Moche did not possess a system of writing, so we are limited in what we can learn about and from them. A large part of what we have gleaned is derived from surviving cultural artefacts, many of which were then unfortunately appropriated by those who followed. What this means is that, sadly, many questions about the Moche, these highly advanced progenitors of Peruvian culture, will remain unanswered.

SHAMBALA

The hidden kingdom of Shambala is described in ancient Tibetan religious texts as a mystical place. Although in geographical terms it is supposed to be located somewhere between the mountains of Tibet and the vast Gobi desert, it is allegedly separated from the world by a spiritual boundary, meaning that only those who are meant to find it will ever reach it. The kingdom has been sought by Tibetan lamas (religious men) for centuries, many putting aside years of their lives in dedicated spiritual preparation.

The Tibetan manuscripts contain detailed descriptions of the secluded land. Maps liken its shape to that of an eight-petalled lotus, with the palace of Kalapa situated in the centre and illustrations reveal that the inhabitants of Shambala are blessed with advanced means of transport such as aircraft and shuttle systems. They also possess sophisticated scientific instruments with which to study the stars.

Contained in the texts are prophecies relating to the rulers and people of this mysterious kingdom. Precise information is given about the reigns of the 32 kings of Shambala, the dates of the various successions being listed in detail. It is also predicted that, over time, the inhabitants will grow in power and enlightenment, gradually acquiring skills such as the art of telepathy and the ability to travel vast distances at great speed. As they develop, the outside world will correspondingly degenerate, becoming warlike and power-hungry, eschewing the spiritual life for material wealth.

The same prophecy explains that in around four centuries' time, a day of reckoning will come about. At this point, the world will have deteriorated to such a point that it will be dominated by a vicious king who, believing that he is omnipotent, will discover Shambala and attack it. In this battle, the 32nd king of the hidden kingdom, Rudra Cakrin, will lead a vast army of the pure and enlightened to victory, heralding an age of perfection.

Those who believe in the existence of Shambala view factors such as the global spread of materialism and the troubled history of the last hundred years or so as evidence of the accuracy of the predictions contained in the ancient texts. However, as the predicted doomsday year is not until 2425, there is a long time to go until we can know for certain whether the prophets have correctly predicted the future.

THE AGE OF THE PHARAOHS

There are perhaps no monuments more immediately associated with the concept of mystery than the great pyramids of Egypt. Although such structures are present all over the world, it is the Egyptian examples that are both the most ancient and spectacular and thus have the power to capture our imagination.

The most evocative pyramid of all is the largest, which marks the tomb of King Khufu at Giza in Egypt. King Khufu, the son of Sneferu and Queen Hetepheres I, was the second pharaoh of the fourth dynasty. Inheriting the throne while still in his twenties, he nevertheless immediately began the planning and construction of his tomb. He became the first pharaoh to build a pyramid at Giza and in so doing began a period of monument building

The pyramids at Giza, Egypt, which were built by King Khufu during a thirty-year period around 2,550BC.

that was to span the ages. The clues offered by the great pyramid offer a tantalizing insight into the exact purpose of this kind of structure.

The great pyramid took well over 20 years to complete, using around 2.3 million individual blocks of stone, weighing up to 2.5 tonnes each. The sheer size of the tomb may well have reflected the great power and respect enjoyed by this particular pharaoh. The entire process of mummification, monument building and ritual burial are aimed at the concept of granting the king a passport to the afterlife. In preparation for this, vast chambers were built within the tomb and filled with an immense variety of riches.

On further examining this pyramid, a number of factors have led many to suspect that there may be some hidden meaning contained within the structure. First, Khufu's personal burial chamber is larger than that of any other pyramid in the world and its construction is of the highest standard. In fact it is so intricate that it contains a small shaft, running all the way from the burial chamber up to the sky in a completely straight line.

The precision of the line is such that some Egyptologists believe it may have been intended as a conduit for the *ka*, or spirit of the pharaoh. It has also been suggested that the line of the shaft from the burial chamber would have aligned with the constellation of Orion at the time of the king's burial and, furthermore, that this pyramid and the two others built at Giza may actually form a representation on Earth of this particular constellation. Support for this theory is provided by the fact that Orion had particular importance for the Egyptians in terms of the afterlife.

There has also been much discussion about the supposed mathematical perfection of the pyramid's dimensions and position. Considering the religious importance of these factors to the Egyptians, these points may be worth considering. Each face of the pyramid is hyper-accurately oriented towards each of the cardinal compass points. The Egyptians used precise geographical north, which is aligned with the spin axis of Earth, rather than magnetic north. This fact demonstrates the Egyptians' advanced understanding of the world and suggests that they were aware that Earth was a sphere that rotated. The position of the great pyramid exactly straddles the 30th parallel latitude, setting it precisely one third of the way between the North Pole and the Equator.

Just as there seems to be a very precise positioning involved in the construction of the pyramid at Giza, so too can a curious alignment be seen in the temple of Amen-Ra at Karnak. Here, doorways to the monument have been built so that they line up exactly along the bearing 26° south of east, to 26° north of west, over the distance of almost one kilometre. This coincides exactly with the position of the rising and setting suns on the days of the spring and winter solstices.

Such factors could be coincidental, but taken together they begin to suggest that perhaps the edifices of ancient Egypt contain some greater significance in their structure. The deliberately huge scale of the pyramids would moreover ensure that they defied the ravages of time and thus carry this message into subsequent millennia. Certainly, many Egyptian monuments would seem to demonstrate the importance to this ancient people of certain times of the year, such as the solstices. The Egyptian calendar also followed a kind of cyclical Zodiac that applied a particular cosmic importance to each particular day. This is in its essence very similar to the ideas expressed in astrology today in cultures all over the world.

The pyramids are a potent symbol of mysticism and inspire great curiosity all over the world. Their true meaning and purpose can only be guessed at, and we will probably never know the real answers. Perhaps what is most important, though, is that the pyramids prompt us to ask the right questions, questions about the power and wisdom of the ancients, the nature of civilization and the mysteries of the universe.

GHOSTLY GOINGS-ON

Chilling tales of brushes with the dead form an integral part of most story-telling traditions. Fireside thrillers, films, fairground rides, tours and innumerable books explore the possibility of the existence of the afterlife and reveal our enduring fascination with the idea of ghosts. Some famous ghosts are said to haunt the area where they died in the hope of seeking justice. Others are said to serve as a warning. Many people who encounter spirits say that they are benevolent, and the ghosts are regarded with affection, but some spirits appear as negative and, occasionally, angry forces.

CREEPY CASTLES

Over the centuries, castles have borne witness to much human suffering, with numerous incidents of incarceration, illness, suicide and murder. Perhaps it is, therefore, not surprising that there should be such a high degree of spectral sightings within their walls.

For many hundreds of years, strange apparitions have been reported at the Tower of London, the oldest palace, prison and fortress of its kind in Europe. The Tower was built by William the Conqueror on ground which, 1,000 years earlier, had been the site of a Roman fort, constructed by the Emperor Claudius. Today, this monument attracts a huge number of visitors, many of whom are lured there in the hope of seeing one of the many ghosts rumoured to stalk its grounds.

During its time as a prison, the Tower was home to many famous inmates, including Queen Anne Boleyn, Guy Fawkes, Thomas More, Princess Elizabeth, Lady Jane Grey and Walter Raleigh. Many of these unfortunate prisoners endured agonizing torture before being executed in the most barbaric way – often they were beheaded, or hung, drawn and quartered. Their heads would then be impaled on spikes on the perimeter walls to serve as a gruesome warning to the public.

There has been a long line of reports of hauntings at the Tower, the first of which were made in the mid-13th century. Construction workers building the inner curtain wall claimed that the ghost of an irate Thomas Becket appeared before them and reduced the wall to rubble by striking it with his cross.

The ghost of the 70-year-old Countess of Salisbury also lingers at the site of the executions, where she met a truly grisly end. Henry VIII had ordered that she be beheaded, but at the last moment she tried to escape her death by running from the block. The executioner chased her, swinging his axe, and eventually hacked her to death. Some have spoken of seeing the execution re-enacted before their eyes, while others have observed the shadow of the fateful axe on the walls in the vicinity.

Of all the sad souls still said to be roaming the Tower, it is the figure of

Anne Boleyn that seems to be the most persistent. This tragic figure was tried and executed for adultery and treason after miscarrying the potential heir to the throne. Her headless body, recognizable from the dress she was wearing on the day of her execution, is reported, even today, to drift from the Queen's House to the Chapel of St Peter Ad Vincula. Here, it leads a spectral procession of dignitaries down the aisle to the site of her final burial place under the altar.

The Salt Tower is the most feared and thus the most avoided area of the Tower of London. Yeomen Warders are reluctant to go near it at night after one of their members was inexplicably strangled. Dogs – who, in common with many animals, seem to have a sixth sense regarding supernatural beings – refuse to go near it, further fuelling intrigue and superstition.

The presence of ghostly apparitions in the Tower was captured on camera as recently as 2003, when a photographer reported strange incidents while attempting to conduct a photo shoot. Bulbs kept blowing and flashes went off unexpectedly. Most eerily of all, when he came to develop the film, he discovered, among the many blank pictures, a photo containing a mysterious ball of light in the centre of the image.

Another famous British tourist attraction, Windsor Castle has been a home to royalty since the 11th century and is still a royal residence today. Over the centuries, it has seen innumerable births and deaths and has been connected with countless legends of witchcraft and treachery.

Of all the spectres rumoured to stalk the castle grounds, those of three kings, in particular, have made their presence felt within the castle walls. The footsteps and groans of King Henry VIII are allegedly heard by visitors to this day, while the ghost of King Charles I, beheaded in 1649 at Whitehall, is also said to roam the grounds, and has been sighted, complete with head, in the library and the canon's house. Sightings of 'mad' King George III, who was incarcerated in the castle before his death, have also been recorded.

Of similar renown in Scotland is Edinburgh Castle, a fortress magnificent in its austerity. Built on the site of a once-active volcano, this almost 1,000-year-old construction has seen an unusual degree of violence and death, factors that could account for the large number of ghostly apparitions in the vicinity. The most famous of these are the figures of the headless drummer and piper who are said to patrol the castle's battlements, still playing their instruments.

In recent years, there have been tales of encounters with spirits arising from a fascinating discovery that was made in the city in the early 1990s. During renovation work, remains were uncovered of buildings buried beneath the existing city. It is known that during the Black Death in 1665 Edinburgh was blighted by a terrible plague that decimated the population. As the disease dwindled, surviving officials deemed it best to build over the top of the old, ravaged city, entombing the affected buildings and any remaining living sufferers under the new constructions. Since this forgotten world has come to light, many people have heard ghostly voices and seen beautiful flashing lights emanating from the subterranean city.

Another Scottish fortress, Glamis Castle, was famously recorded by Shakespeare in his tragedy *Macbeth*. The mysterious happenings at the castle are not restricted to the realms of the theatre, however – many dark deeds and hauntings have taken place within its ancient walls.

Legend tells of the misdeeds of the second Lord of Glamis, whose dalliance with the devil is said to have left its legacy in the brutal acts of violence that ensued. 'Earl Beardie' or 'the Wicked Lord', as he was nicknamed, was apparently a violent gambler and drinker. One evening, unable to find a gambling partner, he is supposed to have announced that he would resort to playing with the devil himself. Moments later there was a knock at the door, and a tall, bearded man dressed entirely in black asked the lord if he still required someone with whom to gamble. When the servants heard shouts and the sound of furniture being flung around the room, one of them crept to the keyhole to try to get a glimpse of what was going on, where he was caught by his master. When Lord Glamis returned to the room, the dark stranger had vanished, taking with him the soul of the gambling aristocrat. He died five years later, and his drunken, tortured spirit is said to still roam the castle, waiting to return to the room to play with the devil.

The castle is also home to the ghost of Janet Douglas, who was the wife of the sixth Lord of Glamis. Following his sudden death, she was accused of murder and witchcraft, even though there was no evidence to this effect. She was put on trial, during which she was found guilty of plotting the murder of the king of Scotland and summarily executed in Edinburgh in 1537. Her spirit is said to wander the halls of Glamis and she is frequently seen praying in the small chapel where she had vainly sought refuge almost 500 years ago.

Could it be that, in common with many other ghosts that inhabit some of Britain's oldest castles, she is seeking justice? Whatever the motives of these spectral beings, they are likely to continue to haunt some of our most ancient monuments, and remain an enduring source of fascination to mankind today.

HEXED HOUSES

Over the years, haunted houses have inspired generations of writers, artists and film-makers and captured the imagination of people of all ages, in every part of the world. By examining the history of these supernatural residences, we can gain a fascinating insight into the identity of their otherworldly inhabitants.

Temple Newsam House in Leeds, West Yorkshire, is an imposing Tudor-Jacobean house set in 1,200 acres of lush, rolling parkland. Dwellings on this site were listed in the Domesday Book of 1086, and in the 12th century the house became the property of the Knights Templar. In the 15th century, it passed to the family of Thomas, Lord Darcy, a friend of Cardinal Wolsey, who became the first of a number of people to build parts of the house that still stand today. Following Darcy's brutal beheading for his involvement in the Pilgrimage of Grace revolt, the house was seized by Henry VIII and given to his niece, the Countess of Lennox.

It was in these spectacular historical surroundings that Henry, Lord Darnley, after whom the most famous room in the existing house was named, was born. Darnley grew up surrounded by political intrigue, eventually culminating in his fateful and turbulent marriage to Mary Queen of Scots, which ended with his mysterious murder.

Following this, the house was requisitioned by Queen Elizabeth I and since then has passed through many royal hands, undergoing several transformations along the way. It has remained a centre of political strife, and Darnley's murder has not been the only one carried out within its walls. Perhaps it is not surprising, then, that 'the Hampton Court of the North' seems to be home to more than just the living.

Numerous spirits have been seen in various parts of the house over the ages, most notably in the Darnley Room, located in the south-west corner of the early Tudor part of the building. Frequent sightings are made of the spirit of a Knight Templar, still on guard after 900 years, and the disturbing spectre of a small boy who is said to appear from inside a cupboard and cross the room, screaming in pain and anguish.

Another ghost to haunt this property on a regular basis is the 'Blue Lady', the spirit of Mary Ingram, whose portrait hangs in the Green Damask Room, and who lived in the property during the 17th century. One night, while returning home in her carriage, the unfortunate woman was attacked and robbed by highwaymen. Although not physically harmed, the incident seems to have damaged her psychologically, for from that point on she became obsessed with concealing her possessions. She roams the house to this day, dressed in a long blue dress and lacy shawl, hunting for her long-lost treasures.

Another former royal residence to see more than its fair share of scandal and intrigue is Cumnor House in Oxfordshire. During the 16th century it was home to Lord Robert Dudley and his wife Amy Robsart. Dudley was a close friend of Queen Elizabeth I and barely left the side of the young monarch during the early years of her reign.

Rumour was rife about an impending royal marriage, seemingly hindered only by the fact that Dudley was already married. In the pursuit of power and royal favour, Dudley abandoned Amy, who was only too aware that she remained the only obstacle to her husband becoming king.

Fearing for her life, she retreated inside Cumnor with just a few trusted servants for company. She became paranoid about her safety, taking great care over what she ate for fear of poisoning and not even venturing out into the beautiful grounds that she loved so dearly.

Despite these extreme precautions, however, Amy could not cheat her destiny. One day, when her staff had left her alone in order to attend the annual fair, she met with tragedy, and when her servants returned from their day out they found her broken body lying at the bottom of the stairs. Slander and calumny ensued, with Queen Elizabeth and Lord Dudley as the prime suspects. The scandal forced the queen to abandon her plans to marry Dudley, as this would have seemed to confirm the rumours. Instead, she made him the Earl of Leicester, and they remained close friends until his death in 1564.

The truth of the mystery surrounding Amy Robsart's death has never been established. Perhaps it is for this reason that there were so many sightings of her restless soul drifting around the stairs where she met her unfortunate end. Eventually, in 1810, the owners decided to demolish the staircase. This had little effect since her sad spirit simply transferred its lonely wanderings to the gardens and parkland surrounding the house. Despite further attempts at exorcism by clergymen, locals to this day claim they see Amy in the vicinity.

Another haunted English residence is Raynham Hall in Norfolk. This ancestral home of the Marquess of Townsend is inhabited by a restless spirit called the 'Brown Lady', whose presence has, over the last 170 years, been felt, seen and even captured on film.

This famous ghost is thought to be the spirit of Dorothy Walpole, sister of Sir Robert Walpole, the first prime minister to live at 10 Downing Street. Dorothy, like Amy Robsart before her, suffered at the hands of a cruel husband, who took custody of her children when she started to show

The famous picture of the 'Brown Lady' descending the stairs where she met her death at Raynham Hall.

symptoms of mental health problems. The unfortunate woman was then incarcerated in a first-floor bedroom and, again like Amy Robsart, died mysteriously after falling headlong down a flight of stairs.

Sightings of this unfortunate soul are well documented, and often involve those who were formerly sceptical of such supernatural activity. One of the most famous cases was recorded in 1835 by Frederick Marryat, a Royal Navy officer and politician's son, who, at the time, was staying at the house in the very room that had served as Dorothy's prison during her final days.

Despite rejecting the allegations about the presence of the ghost, Marryat took the precaution of keeping a loaded gun about his person while in the building. The first two nights of his visit passed without incident, but on the third night an event, witnessed by two other people, was to shake his cynicism to its very foundations.

As the three friends were returning to their rooms one evening, they were surprised to observe a woman entering Marryat's room. The officer challenged the intruder who, in spite of being confronted by a gun, ignored his imperious command, whereupon Marryat opened fire. When the smoke cleared, the three were astonished to find no sign of the expected body. The only evidence that the shot had been fired was a bullet hole in the wall.

Then, almost exactly a century later, this house became the site of one of the most famous photographs to be taken of any supernatural entity. While shooting the property for a feature in *Country Life* magazine, a photographer made an astonishing discovery – one of his pictures clearly showed the outline of a woman descending the main stairway where Dorothy had met her death. Despite rigorous scientific testing, sceptics have been unable to label the picture a forgery. In fact, on the contrary, it seems to prove the existence of the ghost of a tortured soul who continues to haunt her former abode in the endless search for justice.

Further evidence of ghostly activity can be found many thousands of miles away, on the other side of the world in Australia. The Monte Christo Homestead in Junee, New South Wales was built in 1884 by Christopher

Crawley, a local farmer. Today, it is known as the most haunted house in Australia.

Crawley was an intelligent man, who showed immense foresight in building the Railway Hotel at the same time as he built his home. With the Great Southern Railway Line having arrived in the area in 1878, he was able to take advantage of the sudden explosion in the town's growth, and thus his future was assured.

Crawley lived with his wife and family at the Monte Christo Homestead for many happy years, during which time he made improvements to the already impressive structure. Tragedy, however, struck this once happy home in 1910, when Crawley died as a result of an infection. His wife spent the remaining 23 years of her life in mourning, reportedly so devastated by her husband's death that she only left the house on two occasions following the funeral.

In 1948 the last member of the family left the house and it stood empty and desolate until it was bought and restored in the early 1960s. Since that time, its many occupants have borne witness to an extraordinary amount of supernatural activity. Some have seen the spirit of a small boy playing in the gardens, and others have observed a woman dressed in period costume pacing along the balcony. The most frequent sightings, however, are of the Crawleys themselves, in particular the long-suffering Mrs Crawley. She is reported to roam around her former home, barring some from entering the property, and has also been seen in the chapel, wearing her mourning dress and a large silver cross.

Of the many visitors to the house over the years, the vast majority claim to be aware of a mysterious presence there. People speak of feeling uneasy, or of being watched, and report an inexplicable drop in temperature in certain areas of the building. Its current inhabitants say that strange occurences, such as the banging shut of the doors of empty rooms or the sound of footsteps on the carpeted floor of an unoccupied room, are so frequent that they no longer find them strange.

The number and similarity of these accounts lend them real credibility.

As a result, the house has recently been the subject of a paranormal investigation, and was filmed as part of a documentary. The publicization of this investigation and the residence's ensuing widespread reputation have made this old house famous throughout Australia.

HAUNTED CHURCHES

Vast numbers of the deceased are buried every day in churchyards all over the world, and so it is perhaps hardly surprising that many churches contain evidence of ghostly beings, not yet ready to rest. Every year there are hundreds of reports of spectral sightings in these holy houses, some of which have been captured on camera and evade all explanation.

One of the most famous photographs was taken in the picturesque village of Newby, Cumbria, in 1963. It was a quiet day, and the Reverend Kenneth Lord decided that it was an ideal opportunity to photograph the altar, having promised some days before to supply a picture to the village magazine.

He loaded his antique black and white camera, set up the shot and took the picture. Everything appeared normal until he developed the photograph, which clearly showed a tall, hooded, transparent figure to the right of the altar. The reverend gentleman was unable to explain the anomaly and vehemently denied having faked the apparition in any way at all.

Experts analysed the picture to see if any kind of forgery had taken place. However, even after the most rigorous testing, scientists remained baffled. Recent examination using modern technology has further deepened the mystery, as it has shown that not even the latest computer software could produce the same photographic image.

What is the answer to this mystery? Did Reverend Lord possess technological skills far in advance of those we have today? Or could this photograph be evidence of a kind of spirit world, invisible to the naked eye?

A similarly perplexing picture was taken in 1891, during the early days of photographic technology, on the site of Combermere Abbey, Shropshire.

The abbey had a turbulent history – having originally been a 12th century Cistercian monastery. All that remained, following King Henry VIII's dissolution of the monasteries in the 16th century, was the Abbots House and Hall. In the early 19th century, this highly desirable residence, set in 22,000 acres of rolling countryside, was presented to Sir Stapleton Cotton – along with the title Viscount Combermere – as a reward for his many services to his country.

This illustrious cavalry officer had had a dazzling career, having being made governor of Barbados in 1817. While holding this post, he ordered an investigation into the famous mystery of the moving coffins. Despite his best efforts, he was ultimately never able to establish how a number of coffins in a sealed vault could repeatedly move around within the crypt.

The viscount was to come to an unfortunate end 74 years later when he was knocked down and killed by a runaway horse-drawn carriage in his home village. On the morning of the funeral, a cold day in December, a Miss Sybil Corbet decided to bid the viscount's residence a sad farewell and photographed the hall as a memento. This once vibrant place seemed eerily still and quiet when she took the picture and she reported feeling vaguely uneasy. When the photograph was developed, it proved that her sixth sense had been right, for she seemed to have captured on film more than just the spirit of the place.

It is said that if the picture is studied closely, the translucent outline of a head and chest can clearly be seen in the armchair, with an arm resting along the side. This apparition is said to resemble the deceased Viscount Combermere who perhaps, like the photographer, had decided to say one last goodbye to the hall.

Such ghostly apparitions are not confined to the UK, however. Across the Atlantic, in the USA, many strange sightings have been reported, of which perhaps the most famous have occurred at the burial ground of the Westminster Presbyterian Church in Baltimore.

In 1786, members of the church committee decided to build a war cemetery on the site of a former peach orchard, located just outside the city boundary. Word soon spread about the tranquillity and beauty of the site, and soon all the most affluent citizens were building elaborate tombs there to house their deceased. Among these illustrious denizens were 24 generals, four congressmen, most notably, Edgar Allen Poe and his family.

During the first half of the 19th century, Baltimore experienced an increase in population and underwent radical change. Many new buildings were required, and the countryside surrounding Westminster church was soon built over. By 1850, such was the requirement for land that city officials declared that all burial grounds not directly attached to a church had to be relocated to outside the city. In order to avoid obeying this decree, the Westminster committee decided to attach the site to the church by building supporting arches in the vault and erecting walls around the existing pathways of the cemetery. Relatives were allowed easy access to the graves of their loved ones in the catacombs beneath the building.

As time passed, however, the city expanded and Presbyterian worshippers moved elsewhere. Eventually, the cemetery fell into disrepair, and suffered damage at the hands of vandals, vagabonds and body-snatchers. Children, adopting it as a playground, were apparently seen digging up graves and running round the cemetery with skulls on top of broom handles. Could so many sightings and supernatural experiences have been reported at this old cemetery because of the high level of disrespect shown to those buried there?

Of all the spirits to appear at the graveyard, the most frequent visitor is the ghost of Lucia Watson Taylor, who was interred in 1816 at the tender age of 16. There are numerous corroborating eyewitness reports that describe the benign apparition of this girl kneeling in prayer by her own grave.

The shadowy, mysterious figure of a man dressed from head to toe in black has also been spotted in the cemetery for a number of years. Apparently, he is always wearing exactly the same clothing – his head and face are covered by a fedora and scarf, and he holds a stick. Interestingly, he appears annually on 19 January, the birthday of Edgar Allen Poe. Could this be the ghost of the deceased author?

Such is the level of hauntings at this churchyard that it is frequently visited by psychics and ghost-hunters. While all speak of the presence of otherworldly spirits, this would appear to be backed up by investigations using Electronic Voice Phenomenon (EVP). This technology has captured tape recordings of strange murmurs – could these be evidence of communication from 'the other side'?

GHOST SHIPS

For as long as man has sailed the ocean waves, stories of ghost ships have abounded. Whether these horrifying tales are linked to human error, natural disaster or to another cause entirely, the number and frequency of these sightings seem to suggest that spectral vessels do, in fact, exist.

One such story emanates from the famously treacherous waters of the Cape of Good Hope, at the southern tip of the African continent. The year was 1641 and the *Flying Dutchman* was returning to Holland laden with booty following an extremely successful period of trading in the Far East.

As the vessel was approaching the Cape, Captain van der Decken was deep in thought, his mind occupied with the possibility of the creation of a settlement on the Cape to serve as a point of respite for trading ships in the area. Unfortunately, he was so lost in thought that he failed to observe the ominous change in weather conditions – too late, he realized that his ship had sailed straight into the eye of a savage storm.

Despite battling for several hours to stay afloat, the *Flying Dutchman* struck the jagged rocks surrounding the coastline, gouging an irreparable hole in the side. Legend has it that, as the boat sank beneath the waves, the captain, recognizing his impending death, shouted 'I WILL round this Cape even if I have to keep sailing until doomsday.'

Ever since that fateful day, many people – tourists, locals and naval personnel alike – have claimed to see the ghost of the lost ship on stormy nights. Moreover, it is claimed that whoever is unfortunate enough to catch sight of the spectral vessel dies a horrific death shortly afterwards.

One such incident involved the Royal Navy ship, the *Bacchante*, in 1881. Upon rounding the Cape the lookout man and officer of the watch claimed to have seen: 'a strange red light as of a phantom ship all aglow, in the midst of which light the mast, spars and sails of a brig two hundred yards distant stood out in strong relief.' Shortly after the sighting, the lookout fell from the mast and died.

A similar report was made 42 years later by another group of seamen, who recalled a strange light and being able to discern a ship's hull, two masts and a wispy mist in place of sails. Fortunately for them, this sighting did not signify their impending death, and they survived to tell the tale.

Another vessel that has seen a large number of eerie occurrences is the famous cruise liner, the *Queen Mary*. This ship, which was the jewel in the crown of the Cunard fleet prior to the Second World War, was requisitioned by the armed forces on the outbreak of the conflict and converted to carry troops to the front line. It was during one of these voyages, in October 1942, that a horrific accident took place.

The vessel was rounding the coast of Ireland on the final part of its mission, accompanied by six destroyers and HMS *Curacoa*, in case of attack by German U-boats. As a defensive tactic, the *Queen Mary* had been instructed to steer a zigzag course, with the much smaller destroyers and *Curacoa* ordered to stay ahead of the ship in order to avoid being thrown off course by the swell of the larger craft.

The *Queen Mary* was continually making minor adjustments to its course, and it was during one of these fractional modifications that a slight bump was felt in the vessel's engine rooms. As there seemed to be no evident damage, the *Queen Mary* ignored the contact and continued on its way. The minor bump was, in fact, HMS *Curacoa* being broken in half by the enormous bulk of the troop-carrying ship. A horrifying total of 338 out of the 439 crewmen on board the *Curacoa* died as a result of the collision.

After the war it was decided that the ship should be converted into a floating hotel, a purpose it fulfils to this day. In order to undergo the transition, in 1967 the *Queen Mary* made its way to Long Beach in the

USA – and it was at this time that strange incidents started to occur all over the vessel.

One story involves the sighting of a woman wearing a 1950s bathing costume in a part of the ship that was being converted into a swimming pool. Despite the restricted access and lack of water in the unfinished pool, the woman appeared to be about to dive in, whereupon the witness shouted, and the woman disappeared. Records show that a woman fitting the description had drowned in the pool during the previous decade.

Another curious tale concerns one of the watertight doors. One night, a guard on patrol reported hearing sounds coming from behind door number 13 and, oddly, his guard dog refused to go anywhere near the area.

A search of the vicinity revealed nothing. On examination of the ship's archives, it was discovered that, years before, a young man by the name of John Pedder had somehow been trapped in the door mechanism, and ended up being crushed to death.

Several years after the guard's report, a tour guide claimed to have seen the ghostly figure of a young man beside the same door. When shown an old photograph of the ship's crew, the guide was immediately able to identify the man she had seen – it was none other than John Pedder. She was completely unaware that anyone had died in that part of the ship and had no knowledge of the guard's experiences.

Since then, numerous other mysterious happenings have occurred on board the ship. Wet footprints have appeared by the empty pool, eerie noises are heard, and doors open seemingly by themselves. The ship's first captain, who died aboard the vessel, is also said to be seen walking on the bridge.

Perhaps most horrifying of all these stories, however, are the terrible sounds that many have reported hearing below deck. These include the screams of panic-stricken men followed by the sound of metal being torn apart, and the torrent of gushing water. Could this be a ghostly re-enactment of the fateful collision with HMS *Curacoa*?

Ghost ship sightings are not confined to vessels of the high seas, however. The treacherous waters of the Great Lakes in Michigan, USA, have been a watery grave for a large number of craft over the years, and so it is perhaps not surprising that so many ghostly stories abound in this area.

One of the strangest of these tales concerns a schooner, the *Western Reserve*. The ship was the property of financier Peter Minch, who was aboard the vessel with his family when it sank in 1892, taking with it all passengers and crew. Eerily, the vessel can still be seen silently sailing the waters off Deer Park, where it went down. Perhaps even more mysterious, however, is the fact that the tragedy was foreseen in a dream by a Captain Truedell. He saw events take place in such detail that he was even able to instantly identify the body of Peter Minch when it was washed up on shore.

Another strange event is the disappearance – and subsequent ghostly re-appearance – of the *Erie Board of Trade* on Lake Huron in 1883. Moreover, legend relates that a ghost's curse was involved in its fate.

According to records, the captain had ordered an unfortunate crewman to scale the huge mast to sit in the bosun's chair, even though the chair was known to be unsafe. The sailor obeyed orders and subsequently fell to his death. Stories were told, once the ship docked, how, shortly after his fatal fall, the sailor's ghost had started to appear all over the ship. Having left port on its next voyage, the schooner then vanished inexplicably, but, eerily, can be seen to this day still sailing on the lake.

All these tales make chilling reading, and we have to ask ourselves whether such a large number of people simply have imagined seeing these ghostly vessels and their passengers, all of which had met their end so many years before?

BATTLEFIELD GHOULS

Battlefields are the scene of murder, mutilation and mayhem, and so it is not surprising that they are some of the most common arenas for supernatural encounters. Resonances of the mutual hatred felt by opposing armies and the violence perpetrated still seem to echo around the scene of many conflicts. Innumerable visitors report strange phenomena, such as the eerie sensation of being watched, ghostly lights, mysterious cold pockets of air and sightings of the spirits of long-dead soldiers.

One of the most famous battlefields in British history is Culloden Moor in the Scottish Highlands, the site of the last battle to be fought on mainland British soil. The ferocious and bloody fighting that took place on that sodden day in April 1746 lasted a mere 40 minutes, but the effects of the slaughter abide to this day.

The battle was between the Jacobites, under Bonnie Prince Charlie, who were seeking to restore the Stuart monarchy to the throne and government troops, led by Prince William, the Duke of Cumberland. The Jacobites were exhausted, having spent many days marching back from an ineffectual mission to gather more troops and a failed surprise attack on the duke's men. They were also vastly outnumbered and not suited to fighting on boggy moorland.

The battle commenced with an artillery exchange that decimated the Jacobite forces. Bonnie Prince Charlie was notably absent from the front line, so the men were left leaderless and hesitant, with no real battle plan. The slaughter intensified when they finally decided to charge as those troops who had managed to survive the bombardment were then slain by a new, and highly successful, strategy employed by Prince William's troops.

Cunningly, this involved stabbing the Highlander to the right of the man directly faced, and took the Jacobites totally by surprise. It meant that the government troops were able to inflict wounds on their enemy under the right sword arm, an area left unprotected due to the fact that the small shield that they carried, known as a targe, was borne on the left arm.

Those who were not mortally wounded were cruelly slaughtered as they lay on the blood-soaked ground, and those who fled were hunted down and murdered without pity. Bonnie Prince Charlie managed to escape to Italy, but was never able to return to his native land.

Those who have visited the scene of this battle speak of numerous mysterious happenings, particularly on the anniversary of the action on 16 April. For example, they see the ghostly soldiers and hear the clamour of carnage and the clash of steel. Specific sightings of a tall, gaunt Highlander who utters the word 'Defeated' under his breath are described. Others report coming across the spectre of a dead Highland soldier lying beneath a tartan cloth on one of the many burial mounds of the battle site. Birds are said to fall silent in the region of these mounds, and there are also numerous wells strewn across the area that are said to abound with the spirits of the dead, most notably St Mary's Well.

Also ripe with rumours of hauntings is Gettysburg, the site of one of the bloodiest and most infamous battles in the history of the United States. As the location of the turning point of the Civil War, which raged in the country during the 19th century, Gettysburg is of evident importance from a historical perspective. But could it also be of supernatural significance?

Visitors flock to the region every year, some simply to pay their respects to the huge numbers of men who perished there, and others in the hope of an otherworldly encounter. Countless reports of similar incidents in specific areas of the battleground seem to indicate that there may be some truth in the stories, and there is some photographic evidence to suggest that spirits may exist in the vicinity.

The battle, which took place from 1–3 July 1863, was fought between the Army of the Potomac, led by George Gordon Meade, and the Confederate troops, under General Robert E. Lee. A number of strategic skirmishes took place, the most famous of which was Pickett's charge, the Confederate attack against the Union troops.

It was the Union side, however, that was to attain victory in this encounter, which saw the staggering loss of 48,000 lives. When the fighting ceased, the battlefield was awash with blood and echoed with the agonized cries of mortally wounded men from both sides. Worse was yet to come, as huge hogs, let loose by the destruction of containing fences, gorged themselves on the bodies of the dead and dying.

Over the years, visitors to the site of the battle have reported curious occurrences, most notably in those areas of the field that saw the most intensive fighting, such as High Water Mark, Little Round Top and Devil's Den. They have spoken of face-to-face encounters with ghostly soldiers and recall feeling suddenly and strangely cold, as well as hearing the solemn beat of battle drums and the sound of men marching.

Electrical equipment also seems to register the potential presence of supernatural activity, as cameras and recording devices that previously were functioning perfectly normally inexplicably failed to work around the site of the battle.

It is not only on the battlefield of Gettysburg that mysterious happenings take place – local residents also seem to have had their fair share of ghostly encounters. Ghostly soldiers have been seen in those buildings that were standing at the time of the battle, where strange noises and spectral orbs are frequently reported.

In the Eisenhower Elementary School a man's boot prints repeatedly appear on the high ceiling of the first-floor bathroom. Noises are also heard in this room, and tiny green flashes are said to appear when the lights are extinguished.

Gettysburg College is also inhabited by supernatural residents dating from the Civil War. One of the most haunted buildings on campus, Pennsylvania Hall, was used as a hospital during the conflict and as such was inevitably the site of pain, suffering and death.

Students of the college have reported many strange happenings there – for example, the building's lift, rather than going to the selected storey, often inexplicably descends to the basement, where its occupants are suddenly confronted with a particularly gruesome hospital scene.

Others tell of a Civil War soldier who is seen guarding the hospital from his position on the cupola on the roof of the building. Upon noticing the gaze of the living person looking at him, he is said to aim his rifle at the imagined intruder, before disappearing into thin air.

Culloden and Gettysburg are just two of the many battlefields to reverberate with the ghosts of fallen fighters. It seems certain that these sites of conflict will continue to fascinate us, as the extent of the suffering there makes them poignant and ultimately deeply mysterious, places of pilgrimage for mortal man.

ALCATRAZ

Stories of incarceration, torture and thrilling escape attempts have long been associated with the world-famous prison of Alcatraz, nicknamed 'hellcatraz' by its unfortunate inmates. Besides these, however, many mysterious occurrences are reported to have taken place there, and we must ask ourselves whether anything more ominous than a bloody history lurks within its impenetrable walls. Could it be that the island is inhabited by malevolent powers?

Alcatraz – or 'The Rock' – was not always a prison. Many years ago, in the time of the Native Americans, this barren and remote island was known as the 'White Rock', because it was covered with white pelican droppings. It was avoided by local tribes, as it was thought to be the haunt of evil spirits and a possible portal to another, sinister, dimension.

When the Spanish came across the island in the 17th century they named it 'La Isla de los Alcatraces', or 'the Island of the Pelicans', but failed to recognize its importance as a strategic outpost. All this changed in the 1850s, however, when the excellent military defensive potential of the island was finally realized and it became home to a fortress for the purposes of guarding the Golden Gate.

Building work on the fort commenced in 1854. Unfortunately, planners had failed to take into account both the geographical and meteorological factors which were to prove so devastating for many of the construction workers. There was only one landing site on the island and access to this was restricted by strong currents and hazardous weather conditions, notably wind, rain and fog. Once on the island, there was no water or vegetation and, with the supply route being so hazardous, access to essentials from the mainland was severely limited. In spite of the subsequent building of a wooden town around the construction site as well as roads enabling better access, starvation and disease were rife, and huge numbers of workers died in the building of the fort.

Eventually work was completed, and in 1859 the first prisoners were sent to Alcatraz. By 1861 the fortress had been made the official military prison for the entire Department of the Pacific. Prisoners were confined in atrocious conditions, forced to lie head to toe in serried ranks on the hard floor with no sanitary facilities. Not surprisingly, the captives died in their scores from disease.

As time went on, the prison became increasingly notorious, housing military convicts and society's worst criminals. Thieves, thugs, rapists, murderers and escapees from other prisons were sent to the formidable fortress, where they stood little chance of escape. When the increasingly desperate prisoners tried to escape their horrendous conditions, it seemed as if nature was working against them, as fearsome currents would wash them back to the island, or cause them to drown in the icy waters.

By the 1930s Alcatraz had become a maximum-security prison, where only the most vicious and hardened criminals were sent. Men armed with machine-guns stood on guard, although far more inmates met their death as a result of the conditions than through being shot. Once again, nature seemed determined to punish those kept within the prison walls. A cloying, dense fog enshrouded the fort, and icy winds cut through the otherwise impenetrable walls, causing inmates to feel perpetually cold and to fall ill.

Prisoners also had to endure the mental anguish of isolation, which was only heightened by the fact that they could see the lights of San Francisco and hear party boats passing by the island. It was a harsh, brutal life, with violence constantly breaking out among the inmates, and any men who did survive an escape attempt were immediately executed.

The fort ceased to be a prison in 1969, after lying empty for some years, and it remains the property of the Golden Gate National Recreation Area. Every year it attracts thousands of visitors, lured by its brutal history of bloodshed, anguish and hatred. Increasingly, people are drawn to the island by tales of strange occurrences within its walls, many of them coming from officials who frequent the fort, and who are made eerily aware of the resonance of evil. They speak of feelings of dread and of being watched, tormented screams, inexplicable crashing sounds, and the sudden, mysterious closing of cell doors.

Of all of the seemingly haunted areas of the fort, it is cell block D that is the most frightening. This was formerly the solitary confinement area of the prison, and housed the most hardened criminals. Here, prisoners were forced to stand in naked isolation in the freezing darkness for days on end and, as if this was not bad enough, a ghostly presence was rumoured to stalk the area, attempting to strangle the unfortunate inmate.

The inexplicable death of one of the men seems to confirm these reports. This unfortunate prisoner's fate perplexed medical experts at the time of the death, as the position of the bruises on his body revealed that it would have been physically impossible for him to have strangled himself. Could the evil spirit of a long-dead felon have been responsible? Whatever the reason, many inmates of cell block D spent their time continually screaming with terror and eventually went insane.

Today, many Recreation Area rangers refuse to go near this area, which is unnaturally cold and instils dread and horror in those who set foot there. One of the many psychics to visit the island claimed to have felt icy fingers around his neck in one of the cells of D block and he recalled that he was filled with a fear so intense that his hair stood up on end.

In other parts of the prison, sobbing is heard, and the ghosts of inmates appear before rangers and visitors. Sometimes, a strange whistling sound is heard, and the lighthouse, which was demolished many years ago, appears out of the dense fog, casting an eerie light over the troubled island.

Reports of such supernatural encounters are morbidly fascinating to the world at large, and many people continue to be attracted to the island, perhaps hoping to experience the paranormal for themselves. Whether or not the Native Americans were correct in their assumptions about the island being a portal to another world, the site certainly seems to possess considerable negative energies which hold all who visit in their thrall.

CORNISH SPECTRES

Cornwall is an area of the British Isles that is steeped in folklore and mystery. Sinister tales of the deeds of smugglers and sailors, and eerie stories of ghostly beings abound throughout its wild, remote terrain.

Hotels and inns in the region have their fair share of spectral stories. One of the most famous of these is Jamaica Inn, near Bodmin. This hotel was immortalized in Daphne du Maurier's novel of the same name.

To this day, much to the discomfort of the visiting public, a murdered sailor is known to make regular appearances in the bar, seemingly intent on finishing his drink.

The Wellington Hotel in Lanreath is believed to be inhabited by not one, but numerous ghosts. Many have seen the spirit of an 18th century coachman casually strolling past the hotel reception desk before disappearing through the wall. The fact that those who have witnessed the apparition are all in agreement about the exact details seems to imply that there might be some truth to this story.

Another ghost to inhabit the inn is thought to be that of a young girl who flung herself from the ramparts of the hotel's tower while overcome by love's despair.

Yet another seems to attract animals, which eagerly follow an unseen being, the only trace of whom is a shadow moving along the floor.

Another such benevolent spirit is to be found at the site of the ancient manor house at Duporth. Reports stretch back to a century ago when the original house was still standing. Its occupants spoke of a nun, affectionately called 'Flo', who was to be heard striking matches and unlocking cabinets on a regular basis. Although the manor house has long since been demolished to make way for a holiday village, it would seem that Flo is still in attendance. There are many reports of strange happenings – the roundabout in the playground is said to move of its own volition on a windless day, kettles housed in locked and empty rooms suddenly come to life and start to boil and sewing machines spring into action of their own accord. Staff at the holiday site say that if they ask Flo to stop her eerie behaviour the devices fall silent.

Blackaways Cove in north Cornwall is a more sinister site of otherworldly occurrences. This isolated inlet is situated perilously close to treacherous rocks, and has witnessed many shipwrecks over the centuries. Perhaps it is the ghosts of drowned sailors that are responsible for shrouding the region in superstition?

Alternatively, the eerie presence at the cove could be due to a particular drama that unfolded on land above the cove itself.

According to local legend, a father and his two sons once lived on a farm estate on the cliffs. When this man died, he left everything to his eldest son, while the youngest was cut off without a penny. This young man was driven to such a pitch of jealousy that, losing control, he set fire to the farm, totally destroying the property. Ironically, having burned the farmstead to the ground, he then discovered that his elder brother had died the day before, leaving everything to him. Distraught, the man lived out the rest of his days in guilty anguish and remorse. Perhaps the eerie presence at the cove can be attributed to the tortured wanderings of this jealous soul?

The narrow lanes that connect the pretty villages dotted around the coast and countryside also have their fair share of ghostly traffic. A particularly mysterious example of this occurred on the road between Mevagissey and Truro, much to the horror of a motorist, Cliff Hocking.

The terrifying sighting occurred one wet November afternoon while Hocking was driving to hospital in Truro to visit his wife. Upon rounding a bend in the twisting road, he was astonished to discover that he was heading straight towards an old stagecoach, bearing down on him at full speed. He gave a vivid, detailed description of the incident, stating that the coachman wore a wide-lapelled greatcoat, and was standing next to a guard dressed in a red coat and black hat and blowing a post horn.

As the coach and horses sped towards him in a thunder of wheels and hooves, Hocking slammed on his brakes and flung his arms over his head in an attempt to protect himself in the impending collision. However, the crash never happened, and the coach disappeared into thin air.

The stagecoach has since been identified as a mail coach of the type that was used in the 18th century. Such carriages had been introduced to Cornwall in 1796, as part of the nationwide stagecoach service, by a character called Walter Cross who was involved in a number of different activities, one of which was smuggling. Could it have been him at the reins of the coach, fleeing the law with his smuggler's booty? It is unlikely that we will ever find out, but we can be sure that the mysterious Cornish landscape, steeped in myth and legend, will continue to be haunted by the ghosts of its former inhabitants.

PARANORMAL POWERS

Within human society there are groups of people whose remarkable talents and abilities set them apart from the crowd. This is because they are able to break the rules that seem to bind the rest of us – whether these are the laws of physics, such as gravity, or the ability to cross the divide between the worlds of the living and the dead. Various terms are used to describe these people, such as mediums, psychics, telekinetics, or healers and there are innumerable examples of the amazing feats achieved by these people in every civilization and country throughout history.

EILEEN GARRETT

Eileen Garrett was one of the most respected mediums of the 20th century, who possessed remarkable psychic abilities. In one particular séance, she astounded those present – and made headlines around the country – with her uncannily accurate observations. Garrett is also renowned for the assistance she gave to the scientific community in the investigation and explanation of paranormal powers.

Born in 1893 in Beauparc, County Meath, Ireland, Garrett's early years were troubled, as is often the case among those with psychic abilities. Shortly after she was born both her parents committed suicide, leaving the infant Eileen to be adopted and raised by her aunt and uncle. Her gifts became apparent from a very young age. Not only was she able to see auras of light and energy around living things during her childhood, but she also had a large number of imaginary playmates, who took on a very physical appearance to her.

It seems that at this time Garrett was also visited by visions of the dead. She later described the first of these occasions, in which she observed one of her aunts, who lived some distance away, walking up the pathway towards her house with a baby in her arms. The aunt told her that she had to go away and that she was taking the infant with her. The following day it was discovered that this aunt had died in childbirth, along with the baby. Such communication with the dead proved to be an increasingly frequent occurrence throughout Garrett's life.

Having contracted tuberculosis as a child, a condition that was to affect her repeatedly for the rest of her days, Garrett moved to the milder climes of England at the age of 15. Before long, she was married to her first husband, Clive, and she bore him four children. Tragically, her three sons all died very young, two of them from meningitis. Her daughter survived, but by this stage the marriage had ended in divorce.

During the First World War, Garrett met a young officer through her work at a hospital for wounded soldiers and subsequently remarried. Shortly after he left her to join the fighting at the front, she was visited by a vision of her new husband. Two days later she was informed that he had been killed in action at Ypres.

Amazingly, until this point Garrett had not investigated her remarkable powers to any real extent. However, another period of ill health afforded her the time to consider her unusual abilities and she began to attend séances and table-rapping sessions.

She later recalled that it was at one of these events that she started to feel overwhelmingly drowsy and drifted off into slumber. When she awoke, she discovered that she had actually entered a trance, and that during this state her body had been used by the dead as a means of communicating with living people in the room. Shortly after this she made her first contact with the spirit of Uvali, a 14th century Arab soldier who was to become her primary contact with the spirit world at future séances.

After a while, Eileen's growing reputation as a psychic brought her to the attention of a well-known psychic investigator, Harry Price. In October 1930, Price arranged for Garrett to be present at a special séance at the National Laboratory of Physical Research. It was hoped that she would be able to contact the spirit of the famous writer, Sir Arthur Conan Doyle, who had recently died. In preparation, Price arranged for both his secretary and a journalist, Ian D. Coster, to be present to authenticate and document the findings.

It was, therefore, initially disappointing for all concerned when Garrett failed to make contact with Conan Doyle, who had been a spiritualist himself. However, their disappointment soon gave way to astonishment when Garrett proceeded to bring forth the spirit of a Flight Lieutenant H. Carmichael Irwin. It slowly dawned on those present at the séance that this man had been an officer on the *R101*, Britain's largest airship, which had crashed in France two days earlier, killing 48 of its 54 passengers.

Subsequent news reports of the séance came to the attention of a Mr Charlton, who had been involved in the construction of the airship. Intrigued by what he read, he then asked to see the notes of the séance proceedings. These filled him with amazement, as it transpired that, while

French firemen holding up a Royal Air Force flag found among the wreckage of the R101 airship.

in a state of trance, Garrett had produced more than 40 specific pieces of highly technical, confidential information. It would have been impossible, he maintained, for Garrett to have had prior knowledge, or understanding, of such matters.

Charlton was so impressed by these discoveries that he alerted his superiors at the Ministry of Civil Aviation, after which it was decided to hold another séance with Garrett. This time, Major Villiers from the Ministry was in attendance while very specific technical questions were put to Garrett to try to gain further information about the air accident. Detailed answers to these questions were relayed through Garrett, who was able to pinpoint the exact cause of the disaster, even naming the very girder that had failed.

The official court of inquiry examined all of the evidence produced by Garrett during the séance and concluded that it was genuine. Experts declared that it would not have been possible for her to be aware of such precise information about the crash, and that the only explanation was that she had, indeed, communicated with the spirit world. The whole incident was widely taken as proof that such extraordinary powers do definitely exist. This was seen as a real vindication for the spiritualist community, who were often denigrated rather than supported by the establishment.

Garrett differed from many of her fellow mediums in that there were never any overtly theatrical physical manifestations at her séances. Rather than perform table-rapping or materializations, for example, she merely provided the opportunity to speak with the deceased. It was perhaps this simplicity of her approach that caused the establishment to support, rather than condemn, her activities, with many scientists risking their reputations to do so.

Following this widespread acceptance of her abilities, in 1932–33 Garrett agreed to participate in extensive psychoanalytical experimentation at the New York Psychiatric Unit and Johns Hopkins University, USA. In so doing, she revealed her open-minded attitude towards the human need to understand and explain the workings of the paranormal, which she embodied and, indeed, she had a very personal desire to gain a greater understanding of her own abilities. She lectured widely, founded the Parapsychology Foundation in 1951, and contributed her thoughts and findings to several publications, including the *International Journal of Parapsychology*, in 1959.

By the time of her death in 1970, Eileen Garrett was held in high esteem, not just for her skill as a medium, but also for her personal qualities. If she were alive today, she would no doubt continue to be as mystified as the rest of the world as to the precise nature of her psychic powers which, in spite of extensive investigations, remain to this day within the realms of the unexplained.

HELEN DUNCAN

Helen Duncan was the last woman ever to be charged with the crime of witchcraft in the UK. She was found guilty of this crime and imprisoned, despite having produced startling evidence of her genuine psychic abilities during her career as a medium. The most convincing example of this occurred in 1944, during the troubled days of the Second World War.

It is reported that, during one of her séances, Duncan appeared to bring forth the spirit of a sailor who had died while serving in the Royal Navy. The serviceman, who bore the words HMS *Barham* on his hat, told the assembled people that the ship had been sunk while in combat with the enemy. The relevance of this was not realized until the participants of the séance realized that they had been informed of this man's death before the authorities were even aware of it. The sinking of the HMS *Barham* was not announced until several hours after the séance finished and, indeed, it was initially denied that the vessel had been sunk at all.

Later that year, Duncan came under the scrutiny of the law. Fellow spiritualists have since alleged that this was due to the authorities' concerns over the possible risk to military security posed by her extraordinary powers. At that time, the Allied commanders were planning the D-Day invasion of Europe, and security was raised to unprecedented levels. Suspicion about Duncan's activities led to the police arriving at one of her séances, interrupting proceedings and searching the scene. Although they found nothing, she was nevertheless brought to court, where a variety of fraud charges were levelled against her.

In a move that caused some consternation among the public, and outrage among Duncan's community of fellow spiritualists, Duncan was prosecuted under the Witchcraft Act of 1735, and imprisoned. The fact that the authorities were willing to use such an outdated and draconian law suggests a sense of desperation on their part, or at least an ulterior motive. Interestingly, the sentence of nine months that Duncan was given placed her neatly out of the picture until after the D-Day invasion had taken place, and not long after this, in 1951, the Witchcraft Act was repealed and replaced with the more modern and specific Fraudulent Mediums Act.

Once freed from jail, Duncan immediately began working as a medium once more. Yet her involvement with the police was not over, as in 1956 they again suspected her of wrongdoing. This time, they raided her séance in Nottingham while she was in a deep trance. She seemed to react very badly from the shock of being interrupted while in this state, and a doctor had to be called to treat her. Within five weeks of the raid, she was dead.

To this day, there is a campaign to clear the name of Helen Duncan among the spiritualist community, who are enraged by the way she was treated and by the nature of her untimely death. In light of such a large body of evidence of her particular abilities, it seems very hard to refute that she was indeed genuine.

EUSAPIA PALLADINO

Prior to the surge of scientific interest that took place during the Cold War, perhaps no medium had undergone quite such rigorous scientific scrutiny as the Italian psychic, Eusapia Palladino. This renowned spiritualist was investigated by over 50 scientists for more than twenty years and the vast majority of the tests proved that she was, indeed, genuine.

Born in Naples in 1854, Eusapia had a troubled childhood. Her mother died shortly after she was born and, when she was 12, her father was murdered. It was in the year following this incident that her unusual powers began to manifest themselves. While the young Eusapia was attending her first séance, the furniture was said to move towards her and even levitate, an act of telekinesis that was to set the pattern for what was to follow.

The tale of how Palladino rose to psychic prominence is surprisingly convoluted and begins in 1872 in London, long before she had ever set foot there. Here, the English wife of an Italian scientist named Damiani was attending a séance, at which a communication was made with a particular spirit who stated that there was a medium of prodigious talent residing in Naples, and that she was the reincarnation of his daughter. On their return to Italy, the Damianis resolved to seek out this medium. Their enquiries eventually led them to Eusapia Palladino, who was already well known in her community for considerable psychic powers.

In spite of this portentous message, it was still a considerable time before Palladino's talents came to be witnessed by the world at large. Finally, in 1892, word of her unusual abilities reached the famous Italian criminologist Cesare Lombroso, who decided to carry out some investigations into her abilities. After a long series of thorough tests, the initially sceptical Lombroso and his colleagues announced that Palladino was, indeed, a true psychic. This endorsement from one of the foremost Italian scientists of the day caused many learned people from around the world to travel to Italy to witness her demonstrations for themselves, and from this point on, Palladino's fame was assured.

Descriptions of her séances reveal that Palladino was able to perform a remarkable range of psychic activities. Entering a deep trance, she would move furniture around the room, bring forth, out of nowhere, disembodied hands that might touch members of the audience, or convey messages through writing or tapping sounds. Observers noted that the nature of these events seemed to reflect her state of mind at the time, with more violence being demonstrated if she seemed perturbed during the session. Almost all scientific observations indicated that Palladino was an authentic psychic, so there was naturally a great uproar when she was inspected by the Society for Psychical Research in Cambridge, and was declared to be cheating. The scientific community was dismayed, particularly in view of the fact that so many eminent men had given her their backing. However, a subsequent inspection revealed that Palladino was genuine after all.

It is to science that sceptics turn in order to expose sham spiritualists and, therefore, the fact that the scientific establishment of the day ruled so overwhelmingly in Palladino's favour must count strongly towards her credibility. We must also remember the spirit at the London séance who first alerted the world to her powers, as well as her extraordinary early displays of telekinesis. All the evidence points to the fact that Eusapia Palladino was a geniune psychic phenomenon whose mysterious powers are, even today, an endless source of intrigue.

MADAME BLAVATSKY

Madame Helena Petrona Blavatsky was a figure as controversial as she is remarkable, and her writings, views and predictions arouse heated debate and astonishment even today. To many she is considered a powerful psychic, a cultural messenger and even a prophet. As with all controversial figures in history there are those who attempt to debunk her incredible achievements and abilities, but when faced with the evidence, it is particularly hard not to believe that she was genuinely psychic. During her lifetime a wealth of literature by her and about her was created, and she brought about a revolution in Victorian spiritual thinking that affects us all today.

Madame Blavatsky was born in 1831 to a family of aristocrats in Dnepropetrovsk, Ukraine, although she spent most of the rest of her life travelling. The staff and servants of her family home later recalled how unusual she was as a child and how they credited her with possessing powers spoken of in their ancient rustic superstitions. She was reported to be a strange and troubled child, prone to sleepwalking, fits and headaches, all of which are common symptoms amongst those who have experienced visions or otherworldly communications.

By the age of 18 Blavatsky was married to a man much her senior, but she quickly grew tired of him and embarked a life of adventure and travel, leaving her family and country behind. There are numerous versions of Blavatsky's life story, especially concerning the less documented part of her early years. In this time she was alleged to have borne an illegitimate child and to have been the mistress of numerous men. However, despite this behaviour, which was utterly scandalous for the era she lived in, Blavatsky still achieved great fame and respect in society. She was undoubtedly afforded this leeway due to her status as a person who was profoundly different.

Blavatsky spent most of her 60-year life travelling over huge expanses of the globe, studiously absorbing the culture and spiritual thinking of various different sections of humanity. Among the countries she visited were lands as diverse as Canada, Mexico, the West Indies, the USA, Japan, Egypt, Tibet and India to name but a few.

Many of the skills she acquired while on this enlightening world tour were to have a bearing on her later life. She worked at one point with a circus and, at another, as an assistant to a medium who performed séances. However, it was her work alongside Eastern spiritualists that she claimed was the most influential force in her life.

Blavatsky told of how she spent several years in both Tibet and India, studying as the student of great spiritual masters. She claimed that several 'mahatmas' took her into their trust, and that she became their apprentice. Her unique abilities were recognized by these great mystics and she was granted unprecedented access to ancient mystical secrets reserved only for the initiated. It was from these roots that she explained her extraordinary abilities of prophecy and communication with the spirit world.

These Eastern travels were a crucially important aspect of Madame Blavatsky's life for more reasons than this, however, and have left us

Madame Blavatsky, whose extraordinary range of predictions has proved remarkably prescient.

a legacy of knowledge even today. She stated that it was here that she acquired the most important knowledge of her life. With this spiritual learning as her base, she introduced the first real taste of the wisdom and understanding of Eastern religions to the Western world, in particular ideas of karma, reincarnation and the hidden higher powers of the mind.

On her eventual return to the West after her spiritual apprenticeship, Blavatsky propounded the idea of reincarnation – a concept that was totally alien to Western Judaeo-Christian spiritual thinking. She explained how she believed in the spiritual journey of the soul through many different bodies on the road towards perfection. She did not believe in humans reincarnating as animals, but rather that the human soul slowly evolves, improving itself until it can gain extraordinary superhuman powers.

She maintained that a small number of these highly evolved superhuman beings existed in Tibet and India and that they were guiding the fate of the world. The mythical Tibetan paradise of Shambala is said to be inhabited by these luminous superhuman beings who have attained greatness after many reincarnated lifetimes. Blavatsky stated that they were the sole possessors of the hidden 'ancient wisdom' that originated from highly advanced human civilizations of the past. She insisted that they had been guarding this knowledge and using it to benefit mankind.

The nature of what she described endorses certain aspects of Tibetan and Hindu philosophy. Both Tibetan monks and Indian Yogis attempt to reach a higher state of consciousness through dedicated training and the application of their minds through meditation. Many such monks and Yogis are capable of extraordinary superhuman feats as a result of the mystical power they have cultivated within themselves.

Blavatsky was later to crystallize her view of this Eastern spiritual thinking, and combine it with her own sense of mysticism, into a system called the 'Theosophical Movement', which she founded with a number of her followers in 1875. The teachings of this movement are still adhered to by a number of people around the world today. According to Blavatsky herself: 'The chief aim of the … Theosophical society [was] to reconcile all world religions, sects and nations under a common system of ethics, based on eternal verities.'

Blavatsky's aim was unity. It seems that she was seized with a kind of moral fervour, recognizing the inherent wisdom of this ancient and peaceful school of thinking. She realized that for any change to come about in wider society she must publicize this wisdom as much as possible. There is no doubt that this mission benefited greatly from all the publicity she received from her psychic displays.

In some of her demonstrations she was said to have materialized objects such as a cup and saucer. On other occasions she produced written words that were said to originate from the spirit world. The nature of her displays would vary hugely, demonstrating her array of skills and powers. Blavatsky claimed to be able to communicate with her distant Eastern masters by a kind of spiritual telepathy. At one stage she explained how she had seen visions of a tall Hindu who actually materialized before her in Hyde Park, and then became her personal guru and teacher. Claims of this kind were typical of Blavatsky, who liked to create as much mystery around her person as possible to advance her cause.

Some of this has been dismissed by the sceptical as trickery and stage-play, especially as she may have learnt various 'magic' tricks from the performers she worked with. However, there is plenty of other evidence of her abilities that is not quite so easy to dismiss. For instance, her writings contained new explanations of world history that differed massively from the accepted view, and predictions for the future that appear to have the essence of truth within them. Despite seeming outlandish at the time, many of her assertions have been proved true, giving her abilities great credibility.

Blavatsky explained to her Victorian audience that much of the 'ancient wisdom' professed by her Eastern teachers actually originated from the great lost civilizations of the past, such as Atlantis. She first mentioned the lost city of Atlantis in her 1877 book *Isis Unveiled*, which sold out on the day of its publication. In the decade following this, the mystery concerning Atlantis became the talk of the Victorian world, with other authors and thinkers such as Ignatius Donnelly approaching the subject with intense intellectual curiosity. Even today there are scientists and explorers searching for traces of this mysterious lost culture.

In 1888 Blavatsky went into even greater detail in her next book *The Secret Doctrine*. In this book she displays a thorough knowledge of the deep-sea floor, describing details which were far beyond the known science of her day. Notably she asserted that the recently discovered Mid-Atlantic ridge continued under Africa and into the Indian Ocean. This has since been proved true, as the ridge is the boundary of a tectonic plate. What makes this so remarkable is that the Victorians had no idea of plate tectonics, and no means of verifying what she said. Technological advances in more recent times have revealed the extent of Blavatsky's genius.

Although this information may seem unrelated to her other teachings on Theosophy, it is actually tied in completely with her general world view. All that Blavatsky had learned from her masters in India and Tibet was from a store of lost knowledge she referred to as the 'great ancient secrets', which had originated from lost civilizations such as Atlantis or Lemuria, and had been guarded for millennia. Only the initiated were allowed access to this knowledge. Blavatsky claimed that the philosopher Plato himself was an initiate of this secret advanced brethren, which is how he knew about the existence of Atlantis.

Blavatsky's prophecies of events that will befall our own culture make chilling reading. She predicted that there will be: 'a world destruction as happened to Atlantis 11,000 years ago ... instead of Atlantis all of England and parts of [the] NW European coast will sink into the sea, in contrast, the sunken Azores region, the Isle of Posiedonis, will again be raised from the sea'.

Although predictions of doom abound in history, when they come from a character as peculiarly convincing as Madame Blavatsky they cannot be ignored. What is more, scientific revelations and discoveries in the fields of climatology and meteorology have revealed the possibility that she may be right. At present the global climate is warming more rapidly than at any point in history. If this causes the polar ice caps to melt completely, it could have catastrophic ramifications for the world. Global sea levels could rise by several metres and low-lying areas of land, such as England or Holland, would be inundated, fulfilling the prophecy.

Blavatsky's predictions for the Azores also have definite potential to be fulfilled. The Azores is a particularly active geological area, with plenty of volcanic and tectonic activity. Although we cannot say that Blavatsky is correct, and land will rise from the ocean, she managed to pick one of the places in the world that this is most likely to happen. It is unlikely that she could have deduced this scientifically at the time, so we must assume that she gained this information from some supernatural origin.

Once again there is a mystery based on the inexplicable possession of advanced knowledge. When civilizations, tribes, or even individuals possess knowledge that is in advance of the science of the day, serious questions are posed about its origins. It becomes even more intriguing if they claim that this knowledge originates from a time before civilization is even believed to have existed. How could this knowledge exist without the prior existence of an advanced civilization such as Atlantis?

There is much about Madame Blavatsky's life and achievements that it seems impossible to answer fully. Yet there is the unmistakable ring of truth in much of what she said. The peaceful pursuit of meditation and spiritual advancement in Tibet still amazes many in the West, just as it did the audiences of Madame Blavatsky in the 1800s. Scientific predictions for the future seem to concur with some of her more doom-laden prophecies, and many of her assertions were proved true after her death, leaving us to wonder how she came to know such details. Lack of a better explanation means we must accept that she possessed these 'ancient secrets', and that she was one of the most amazing and mysterious characters in recent history.

JEAN DIXON

Jean Dixon was a psychic, clairvoyant and astrologer who, during the course of her life, made a large number of predictions, with varying degrees of accuracy. One prophecy about which she was entirely correct, however, was her foretelling in 1956 of the assassination of President Kennedy, several years before it actually happened. It was only after this event that the world really started to pay attention to her remarkable psychic abilities.

Dixon was born in 1918 and, long before her famous prediction, had been working in the realms of the paranormal, using her powers to prophesy world events. She would foretell the future by means of dreams, in which spirit helpers would impart information to her. This method of prophecy is not uncommon, having been shared by a number of psychics over the years, but it is not the most reliable means of predicting the future as there can be confusion over the interpretation of certain visions.

Dixon's prediction of the Kennedy assassination was, indeed, initially vague – in fact, she did not at first actually name Kennedy as the victim. However, in subsequent predictions, she added more details: she foretold that a Democrat (which Kennedy was) would win the election and that Kennedy would either be assassinated or would die in office. Moreover, she backed up these predictions with a timescale that also proved to be correct.

Although Dixon is best known for her pronouncement on the Kennedy assassination, this was not the only event that she accurately foresaw. She also predicted other notable historic happenings, such as the Soviet Sputnik launch in 1957 and the Apollo rocket disaster that killed several American astronauts in 1967. In addition, she foretold that in the spring of 1989 the world would witness a shipping accident – and the *Exxon Valdez* oil disaster did occur at this time.

Some of Dixon's other prophecies were not quite so accurate, however. She wrongly predicted, in line with early thinking, that the Soviets would land on the moon before the USA, but of course the reverse happened.

She also mistakenly foresaw an apocalyptic 1980s, in which a devastating meteor strike would hit Earth.

Occasionally, Dixon made a prediction that came very close to being reality, such as her prophecy that a third world war would commence in 1958. Although such a conflict did not actually take place, this period of our history was overshadowed to a large degree by the imminent threat of nuclear war.

Dixon also told of a plague that looked likely to descend on the USA during the late 1970s – while this was of course inaccurate, some have suggested that she may have been catching a future glimpse of the arrival of AIDS in the Western world and its devastating effects on public health.

Many have wondered whether it is possible to credit Jean Dixon with psychic abilities when the verity of her predictions has varied so much over time. Her advocates would argue that the future does not actually run along a set course, but is flexible, and that there are numerous possible realities. Dixon, they maintain, simply presents us with one of these potential scenarios. If this is the case, then it would certainly go some way towards explaining how she was so very nearly correct in her predictions of a third world war.

It is certain that debate will always surround figures such as Dixon, because of the inexplicable nature of their amazing powers. Believers will see patterns of truth in the psychic's predictions, while sceptics will continually point out their inaccuracies or ambiguities – it has to be said, however, that even the famous Nostradamus was proved wrong on some accounts, but he is still classed as one of the world's genuine clairvoyants.

As long as mankind exists, there will be a desire to know the future before it actually happens, and it seems that certain special people, with extraordinary gifts, will be able to divine these truths, defying the very laws of time in order to do so.

NINEL KULAGINA

During the Cold War, each side conducted extensive secret research into any area that might give them an advantage over the other. With no subject deemed too unusual to be exploited, both the CIA and the KGB investigated the possibility of using paranormal powers, such as telepathy, for intelligence-gathering purposes. Anyone demonstrating special psychic abilities was seized upon and exploited in the quest for victory.

Ninel Kulagina was one such character. She was a housewife from St Petersburg who was studied by the Soviets for more than ten years because of her paranormal abilities.

During this time she revealed her amazing powers of telekinesis – the ability to move objects by the power of the mind alone. The fact that Kulagina was investigated for such a long period of time seems to indicate that she was nothing other than entirely genuine.

Film footage still exists of Kulagina causing a compass needle to move by focusing energy through her fingertips. Another of her displays of telekinetic ability was to move matches across a table, or to cause a pile of them to collapse purely by the power of a concentrated stare.

But it is the later displays of her remarkable talent that reveal why the authorities were so interested in her powers. In one experiment, an egg was cracked into a saline solution, and she proceeded to separate the yolk from the white by her powers of kinesis.

In another demonstration which was particularly sinister, Kulagina is said to have stopped the heart of a frog from beating, purely by the power of her mind. To the Cold War scientists, this must have been an incredibly exciting breakthrough in human mental ability and this aptitude would have presented all sorts of horrific possibilities to men who were determined to emerge victorious from this most sinister of global conflicts. Performing these incredible feats took a heavy physical toll on Kulagina, and it is this that apparently persuaded the Soviet doctors of the authenticity of her feats.

After she had demonstrated her telekinetic prowess, she reported having experienced a sense of hot energy running up and down her spine and emanating from her hands. During this time, her pulse would apparently race to over 200 beats per minute – the equivalent of doing strenuous exercise, and she is even reputed to have lost weight through such a display. The activities would also affect her blood pressure and she spoke of feeling dizzy and exhausted for several days afterwards, experiencing headaches and blurred vision. Eventually, she was forced to end her involvement with the research after suffering a heart attack, no doubt brought on by her exertions.

Sceptics have argued that all the evidence that exists about Kulagina could have been nothing more than a huge conspiracy on the part of the Soviet powers to alarm the Western world, especially as, during the Cold War years, each side went to a great deal of effort to deceive the other over the extent of the scientific progress being made. Perhaps this is just one more example of such an attempt.

It is impossible to know for sure what secret scientific discoveries were actually made during the era of the Cold War, but there is certainly some very convincing evidence to suggest that Ninel Kulagina was possessed of very remarkable, and mysterious, powers.

DANIEL DOUGLAS HOME

Daniel Douglas Home is considered by many spiritualists to be one of the most gifted mediums of all time. During his unusual career, he demonstrated his psychic prowess on countless occasions and is remarkable for the incredible range of his ability. Whereas most spiritualists tend to specialize in the demonstration of a particular type of paranormal activity, nothing seemed beyond the reach of Home's amazing powers.

Home was born in 1833 in Edinburgh, Scotland and, in common with many spiritually gifted people, his talents first manifested themselves during his childhood. His aunt described how, even as an infant, his cradle could be seen to rock itself, unassisted. As a child, he experienced some significant psychic events, and at one stage is said to have seen a vision of his mother that coincided with her death in another city. Such remarkable powers could not protect him from illness, however, and he was a very sickly child. At the age of nine, he moved from Scotland to Connecticut, USA, to live with his aunt, and it was here that he was diagnosed with tuberculosis.

One of the results of this condition was that Home's childhood was a particularly solitary one, during which time he came to believe that he was surrounded by the spirits of the dead. In fact, he would maintain throughout his life that he was supported by certain spiritual benefactors, and that it was these beings that were responsible for his paranormal displays.

The young Home's fascination with the supernatural and the strange happenings of his early years worried his God-fearing aunt, who believed that he must be possessed by the Devil. Sadly, while he was still in his mid-teens, he was cast out of her house, and from this time on was forced to seek his fortune in the only way he knew how – by working as a professional medium. He would often be offered board and lodging by a patron in exchange for the performance of séances and rituals, at which he would demonstrate his impressive abilities.

Home's repertoire was huge – apart from communicating with the deceased, he would also conjure up from nowhere whole arrays of spectral lights and music. Another of his skills was his extraordinary ability to shrink himself in size, or elongate his body, a phenomenon that was witnessed, and verified, by several people at once.

It was perhaps his displays of telekinesis, though, that were the most remarkable. At several séances, Home caused tables and chairs to move of their own accord and on one occasion he was able to levitate a table to such a height that he could walk beneath it. He maintained, however, that these demonstrations could not actually be classed as telekinesis, for the actions stemmed not from the power of his own mind, but from the actions of friendly spirits with whom he was able to converse easily.

Home made it publicly known at this time that he believed the vast majority of mediums to be fraudulent, and so he took measures to prove that, unlike them, he was genuine. In contrast to other practitioners of the time, Home would conduct his séances in well-lit rooms, or even out of doors. When he demonstrated his ability to move items of furniture, he would challenge the audience to take hold of his hands and feet to prove that he was not touching anything. Many found his displays utterly convincing, particularly those in which he would summon up spirit hands that would then either touch members of the séance, or write out personal messages for them.

Despite such public demonstrations of his talents, it was not until 1852 that Home's career, quite literally, took off. In a display that seemed to set him apart from his fellow spiritualists, Home showed how he was able to levitate off the ground for a prolonged period of time. According to the account of a journalist, F. L. Burr, who witnessed the event, Home levitated no fewer than three times, and on the last attempt actually rose up to touch the ceiling. Home later asserted that the levitation should be attributed to the power of his spirit companions, who had chosen to lift him into the air in this way.

Home's fame spread far and wide, and he set off on a European tour, eventually reaching Russia, where he married. During his travels, he performed séances for some of the leading figures of the day, notably Emperor Napoleon III of France and the Empress Eugenie. Both were amazed by his abilities. At one stage, Home even appeared to make contact with the deceased Napoleon Bonaparte, who signed his name on paper. The emperor was enormously impressed by this, announcing to all that the handwriting was genuinely that of Bonaparte himself.

Arguably the most famous and impressive of Home's feats was performed in London, at the home of Lord Adare, in 1866. Apparently without warning, Home slipped into a trance and began to levitate. He then proceeded to float out of one of the open windows before drifting back in through another. This demonstration ensured Home's popularity and fame, especially as the assembled audience was possessed of considerable credibility and influence.

What is clear is that Home was a supremely talented individual. Some sceptics have asked, however, whether his skills as a medium were genuine or whether his abilities lay more in the area of deception. It has been suggested that Home may have induced some powerful kind of mass hallucination in his audiences through the power of suggestion.

Nevertheless, when one takes into account the consistency of his displays, the huge numbers of people convinced of his authenticity and the lack of any evidence to the contrary, it seems highly unlikely that Home was anything other than a true psychic.

Home was so confident of his own abilities that he agreed to subject himself to some rigorous investigations. Sir William Crookes, a well-known scientist of the day with a particular interest in spirituality, studied Home's activities over a two-year period. During this time, Home apparently managed to make an accordion play while it was sealed inside a cage which had been specially designed by Crookes to block out the magnetic energies that he believed were the root of Home's power.

Finally, Crookes was forced to admit that he could find no scientific explanation for Home's remarkable powers.

At this point, his recurrent tuberculosis forced Home to retire. His powers had not only been displayed and witnessed, but they had been inspected scientifically and there is still no explanation that is more plausible than his own. He was indeed a uniquely gifted individual, and an astonishing manifestation of the latent powers of human consciousness.

RASPUTIN

The story of Rasputin is remarkable, with the events of his life exceeded in peculiarity only by the inexplicable circumstances of his death. A healer and self-proclaimed holy man, as well as the most unlikely of statesmen, he enjoyed incredible influence over the rulers of Russia. The reason for his achievements is still not fully understood, but the most likely explanation seems to be that his powers lay within the realms of the paranormal.

The real name of the man who came to be known as Rasputin (the word means 'debauched' in Russian) was Grigory Yefimovich Novykh. Born in 1865 into a typical Siberian peasant family, he could never have envisaged, in his early years, how much he would go on to accomplish in his life. When he was about 18, Rasputin underwent a religious experience and decided to enter the monastery at Verkhoture, where he stayed for some months. Despite his famous soubriquet of 'the mad monk', however, Rasputin never actually became a genuine monk, perhaps because he was illiterate and unable to read the scriptures for himself. Whatever the reason, it is unlikely that any monastery would have been able to contain for long such an unusual character as Rasputin.

While at this monastery, Rasputin became familiar with the Khlysty religious sect – which mixed its own brand of mysticism with a degree of sexual hedonism not often found in the Church, and which had actually been banned in Russia on heretical grounds. In spite of the fact that he was married, Rasputin launched himself into this world of fornication with considerable enthusiasm, even holding orgies in the marital home. At this time he was beginning to be aware that he might possess some unusual powers, and believed that these could be directly attributed to his sexual indulgences – for this reason he took part in these excesses at every opportunity.

Rasputin went on to father three children by his wife, and probably many more by other women. Yet a family was not enough to keep Rasputin in one place and he wandered far and wide, slowly gathering a reputation as a healer and clairvoyant. He had developed an unusual ability to cure ailments without even having to make a diagnosis, almost as if he detected the nature of the problem through psychic means alone. He travelled as far as Mount Athos, in Greece, and Jerusalem, where he demonstrated his skills to the religious dignitaries, to great acclaim. And so he established his reputation as a 'staretz' (the term for a self-proclaimed holy man and faith healer). Rasputin was not the first illiterate man devoid of formal religious training to follow this path, but he was remarkable in the level

Rasputin in 1910 with his monk's garb and intense gaze.

of the success he enjoyed – which was probably the result of the force of his personality and the incredible results he achieved. Needy people would travel great distances to meet him, rewarding him for his services with gifts or money.

After some time spent travelling, Rasputin returned to his family village where his fame had spread far across the region. It was here that he experienced the vision that was to alter not only the course of his own life, but arguably would have an enormous influence on the history of the whole world. While working in the fields one day, Rasputin apparently saw an apparition of the Holy Mother, who spoke to him and said it was his duty to help to save the life of the young Tsarevich (the prince) Alexis.

The Tsarevich was suffering from haemophilia, which can cause fatal bleeding from even a small cut or bruise, as it prevents the blood from clotting. This hereditary disorder – remarkably common among the European royal families because of their history of intermarriage – had no known cure, and the Tsarevich was in very grave medical danger.

Rasputin travelled to St Petersburg to carry out this mission, although it was to be a while before his influence was felt. By this time, Rasputin had come to the attention of the nobility, some of whom recognized him as a man of God and a person of considerable and inexplicable personal power. Others, however, despised him for his lewd conduct, and considered his claims to be a holy man as nothing short of scandalous. Yet the fact that Rasputin was so removed from the nobility, coming as he did from uneducated peasant stock, meant that he remained a remote figure to them and was not initially perceived as any kind of a threat.

Rasputin lived in St Petersburg for two years before he came to meet the royal Romanov family. He had by now become famous for his lechery, and was extremely popular with Russian noblewomen, with whom he enjoyed many scandalous liaisons. Nonetheless, his success as a powerful religious healer became known to the Tsar and the Tsarina, and in 1906 they summoned him to see them, hoping that he might be able to cure their sickly son. They had to take Rasputin into their personal confidence, for the

Tsarevich's illness was shrouded in secrecy because it might have threatened the prince's right to succession, if it ever became known to the public.

The decision by the Tsar and his wife to invite Rasputin into their lives cannot have been taken lightly, but was to prove fruitful. Through methods impossible to understand, Rasputin appears to have successfully brought to a halt the bleeding of the Tsarevich. This amazing feat rendered him indispensable to the royal family and it would eventually make Rasputin one of the most powerful men in Russia. On leaving the palace after healing the young prince, Rasputin gave one of his famous predictions. He warned that the destiny of the Romanov family was irrevocably linked to that of his own, a prophecy that, with hindsight, turned out to be perfectly correct.

The Tsarina Alexandra grew increasingly close to Rasputin, feeling indebted to him for the service he had performed in healing her young son. She was convinced that his power was a gift from God, and that he had been sent in answer to her prayers. This seems to have been corroborated by Rasputin's own account of his vision. Meanwhile, Rasputin's affiliation with the royal family was causing his influence within the Church to grow. After a while, he came to enjoy such power that he was able to replace those who were against him with his own supporters, gradually eroding any opposition.

Yet Rasputin's support was far from universal. The predilection for alcohol and sexual deviancy that had earned him the name 'Rasputin' had also earned him enemies – since many Church members and noblemen were absolutely appalled by his behaviour. They were also very concerned about the growing influence exerted by Rasputin over the Tsarina, and the rumours that the pair had become lovers – as was Tsar Nicholas himself.

Yet the Tsarina would hear nothing against Rasputin. As far as she was concerned, he was just an illiterate peasant who had succeeded where everyone else, royal doctors, holy men and healers alike, had failed. Little is known about exactly how Rasputin healed the sick child, although many have surmised that it may have been through a form of hypnosis.

The extent of Rasputin's personal power within Russia was to reach its peak in the years before the First World War, and from 1911 onwards he was permitted to appoint his own ministers within the Imperial government. At this time, the Romanov family was becoming dangerously detached from the Russian people, and was shielded by the nobility from the pre-revolutionary feeling that was brewing in the country.

In 1915 Tsar Nicholas took personal control of the Russian armed forces that were fighting in the First World War. Tsarina Alexandra was left in sole command of the country and she immediately appointed Rasputin as her personal advisor. This made Rasputin the effective leader of Russia, an incredible feat for a man who was born a Siberian peasant. Could this have been due simply to the magnetism of his personality, or was Rasputin in possession of psychic powers that enabled him to rise to power in this way?

The evidence certainly seems to suggest that Rasputin had powers that were well beyond the abilities of most people. In addition to his well-documented and proven healing ability, there is evidence of his remarkably accurate predictions for the future. He even managed to successfully foresee his own murder, although he was unable to prevent it.

A group of disaffected aristocrats who deeply resented the power that Rasputin had acquired were intent on killing him and returning power to the nobility. The group of conspirators was led by Prince Felix Yossupov, who invited Rasputin to his home under the pretext of meeting his wife Irina, a woman famed for her beauty. Rasputin accepted the invitation and travelled to the palatial home of the prince, where he was warmly received. The conspirators planned to poison Rasputin with cyanide, which they concealed in some cakes and Madeira wine. Cyanide is one of the deadliest substances known to mankind, and its effects are almost instantaneous. However, these men soon discovered that the extent of Rasputin's powers was greater than anyone could have imagined.

Prince Felix engaged Rasputin in conversation, and persuaded him to try some of the cakes. Although Rasputin's preference was for wine, out of politeness he ate a couple, washing them down with a good measure of Madeira. The prince watched in amazement as Rasputin appeared to shrug off the effects of enough poison to kill six men. At this point, the prince withdrew temporarily to confer with his fellow conspirators who were all mystified by Rasputin's apparent imperviousness to poison. Prince Felix was then presented with a pistol, and told to shoot his unsuspecting guest, whereupon he returned and shot Rasputin in the chest from point-blank range.

Believing Rasputin to be dead, the conspirators gathered over his body to observe their handiwork. At this point, Rasputin is said to have been roused from apparent death and forcefully grabbed hold of them. The men had to beat and stab him in order to free themselves. Amazingly, Rasputin is said to have pushed them off and attempted an escape. He was then shot a second time before being bound with ropes. To be sure they had killed him this time, the assassins then dragged him to the icy Neva river and threw him in.

The Tsarina was distraught by the loss of Rasputin, realizing what this meant for her son, as well as for her, and she demanded that a search be carried out. When his body was recovered, an autopsy was performed, which established that the cause of his death had been drowning. However, it appeared that, remarkably, he had managed to break his bonds and so, no doubt, had come very close to escaping from the river.

This kind of resilience seems beyond human comprehension. Rasputin was poisoned, shot, beaten, stabbed and drowned. Any one of these acts would have been enough to cause the death of a normal man. Surely this was irrefutable evidence of Rasputin's mysterious powers?

To further add to the intrigue and provide yet more proof of Rasputin's extraordinary abilities, it was discovered that he had predicted his own demise in a letter to the Tsarina, a communication that also contained a dire prophecy for the Romanov family.

In the letter, dated 7 December 1916, Rasputin stated that he did not expect to live to see the New Year, a prediction that proved to be correct, for he was murdered only nine days later. The letter also specified that, should he be killed by a common man, then the family of the Tsar would survive, but – chillingly – should he die at the hands of a nobleman, the Tsar's family would all be dead within two years and, furthermore, that no nobleman would live in Russia for at least 25 years.

Only a few months after the death of Rasputin, the Bolshevik revolutionary forces overthrew the Romanov family and the entire system of Russian nobility. Within two years, the entire royal family had been assembled and killed, providing absolute and bloody proof that Rasputin's last chilling prediction had come true. The Bolsheviks also dug up and desecrated Rasputin's grave and burned his corpse, such was the strength of feeling he had generated in the country.

Although Rasputin is now famous only for his association with the Tsar and Tsarina, it should be remembered that he achieved that position as a result of his great success as a healer. He had spent several decades curing people who were sick and helping those who were uncertain about what the future held for them. What lay at the root of his amazing powers is still unclear – Rasputin himself claimed that his abilities were religious in origin, but his personal conduct would seem to suggest that they were simply an innate gift of his own. Whatever the explanation, this colourful Russian figure looks set to remain a source of intrigue to the world for the foreseeable future.

JOSE ARIGO

During his lifetime Jose Arigo became renowned for his inexplicable psychic talents, which he used to great effect in healing the sick and injured. Indeed, many of his actions were even proclaimed as miracles by his admirers. Sadly, however, his attempts to use his amazing healing powers for the good of mankind were eventually cut short by his imprisonment, when the authorities ruled that his activities were contrary to the law.

Born in 1918 into the peasant class of Brazil, Arigo could never have anticipated the level of international fame he would eventually enjoy as a result of his unusual gifts.

He first became aware of his abilities while visiting a dying relative; the whole family had assembled to bid their farewells to the woman who was suffering from a life-threatening tumour. However, as the priest read out the last rites, Arigo recounted how he felt strangely compelled to take action. Seizing a knife from the kitchen, he cut into the woman and removed the tumour on the spot. Amazingly, she made a rapid recovery, and it was after this that Arigo's community realized that they were fortunate enough to have a remarkable psychic healer in their midst.

Such was the poverty in Arigo's neighbourhood that there was very limited access to doctors and medicine. It was not surprising, therefore, that the news of his healing ability spread rapidly, and soon he was being asked to treat large numbers of people. Although initially reluctant to put others at risk by operating on them, Arigo quickly discovered that he was able to repeat the success of his first operation on numerous occasions.

Although such healers have been known to exist in other communities, particularly in the Philippines, rarely has this talent been used with such success, or without recourse to hidden methods. Many of these healers have claimed that they are able to heal the sick because they are somehow blessed, often seeing themselves as conduits for the Holy Spirit. In contrast, Arigo's explanation for his healing powers was an unusual one, as he attributed his skills to the fact that when he was operating he would become possessed by the spirit of a deceased German physician, Dr Adolphus Fritz.

It is difficult to find an alternative explanation for Arigo's remarkable abilities, since he was very poorly educated and certainly had no medical knowledge whatsoever. The only other possibility is that Arigo invented the story of Dr Fritz in order to deflect attention away from the incredible powers that were actually entirely his own. Whatever the truth, Arigo continued to credit the success of his work to the spirit of Dr Fritz throughout his entire life.

Arigo had practised his healing on a large number of people before he came to the attention of the authorities. The medical establishment had serious concerns about the unsanitary nature of his operations and his complete lack of any medical qualifications. Eventually, in 1936, he was arrested for the illegal practice of medicine, after which he was fined and sentenced to eight months in jail. The establishment was not prepared, however, for the huge level of public support for Arigo – the extent of which eventually caused the president of Brazil to step in and offer him an official pardon.

Almost 30 years later, however, in 1964, Arigo was not so lucky, and he was forced to face his sentence. Although the prosecuting judge, Filippe Immesi, was amazed by a demonstration of Arigo's powers, he was forced to conclude that Arigo was nevertheless breaking the law and sentenced him accordingly. While in jail, Arigo still continued his healing practices, believing at this stage of his life that it was his mission to help as many people as possible.

Some time later, Judge Immesi visited Arigo in jail, where the ensuing episode impressed him so much that he subsequently wrote an account of what he witnessed. He described how he had seen Arigo perform a cataract operation on a woman's eye with a pair of nail scissors. Despite the fact that the operation was conducted while the patient was fully conscious, she displayed no signs of pain. No type of disinfectant or antiseptic was used, Arigo merely wiped the scissors on his shirt before cutting into the woman's eye. After he had performed the operation, Arigo said a short prayer before pronouncing that the woman was cured.

Arigo died following a car accident in 1971. In the course of his lifetime, he had healed many thousands of people who, without his intervention, would surely have died.

Modern science is unable to offer an explanation as to how Arigo was able to practise with such an astonishing degree of success, often using in his surgery whatever unlikely implements came to hand at the time. One suggestion is that he might have been using the placebo effect on his patients in the same way as that practised by African witch doctors. These remarkable people trick patients into thinking they have been healed and, because the patients' belief is so strong, they go on to make a full recovery.

However, this method could not explain the incredible level of success that Arigo managed to sustain over so many decades. Belief in his power of healing will take many years to fade.

SEERS AND ORACLES

The desire to predict the future is deeply rooted in human nature. People have always been fascinated by the art of prophecy and throughout the ages have attempted to discern what the future might hold for them. Sometimes they try to achieve this by consulting an individual who possesses the unique ability to see into the future – a seer or an oracle.

There are many different methods of divination, which are practised by societies all over the world. Belief in the power of the prophet is strong, as case after case demonstrates that there is some truth behind this mysterious phenomenon.

THE *I-CHING*

The *I-Ching* or *Book of Changes* remains as important today as it was when it first appeared between 5,000 and 8,000 years ago. Containing the founding principles of Chinese philosophy, this book, together with the Bible and the Koran, is one of the most studied works in the world and is revered for the great insights held within its pages.

The *I-Ching*, which represents a guide to divination and moral counsel, is central to Chinese and other Asian cultures. The study of this book and the basic Taoist principles that underpin its philosophy also form a major part of the study of feng shui, Chinese medicine and most martial arts. By interpreting the *I-Ching*, key decisions about war, love, business and many other personal and political issues can be made.

Taoist principles dictate that within the universe there exists the unknown – this is called the Tao and is represented by a symbol that incorporates the basic universal polarity of the yin and the yang. These two universal forces are united in a perpetual motion of change, and represent the notion that duality and polarity are constantly in flux – nothing is either solely good or solely bad, and all things are in continual motion.

For the Taoists, true virtue arises as a result of a balance and harmony with the universe, a notion that is also evident in Buddhist beliefs. The *I-Ching* derives its form and usage from these principles of yin and yang, the yin being represented by two short lines, the yang by a longer, more solid line.

The earliest records of the practice of 'wisdom divination' in China involved not only the reading of cracks on bones that had been cast into a fire, but also the interpretation of the pattern of cracks found on a tortoise shell. These cracks contain parallels with the arrangement of the yin and yang lines, and on the first tortoise shell the layering of these lines formed eight trigrams.

These trigrams are representative of the eight primal forces of the universe. When multiplied by eight, they represent all possible interactions of these forces with each other. These 64 line figures, representing reality

Careful manipulation of the straws produces a pattern that denotes a sequence of hexagrams.

on all levels, are known as kua. The *I-Ching* contains a chapter for each of these possible outcomes, explaining the meaning of the patterns and providing an insight into the future.

Some believe that the first person to recognize and understand this 'line symbol system' of eight trigrams on the shell of a tortoise was Fu Hsi, the legendary first emperor of China. Other stories relate that Fu Hsi first noted this system, not on a tortoise shell but on the side of a dragon horse as it rose out of the Yellow River. The markings were recorded as the Ho Tu, or 'Yellow River Map', and interpreted according to an early symmetrical arrangement of the eight trigrams. This system then went on to be modified by another mythical emperor, Yu, after seeing a similar pattern on the shell of a tortoise in the Lo River. This 'Lo Shu' map was then interpreted according to a later asymmetrical system that incorporated the four seasons and five elements, and refers to the order of change in the manifest world.

Whichever is correct, both stories agree that the next modification of the system occurred in the Shang dynasty, between 1766 and 1121BC. Wen Wang, usually referred to as 'King Wen', was a powerful feudal lord who was imprisoned and sentenced to death by the Shang emperor, Chou Hsin. While languishing in prison, he is said to have studied the trigrams and combined them to form hexagrams and the kua. He then named and organized the 64 hexagrams into their present arrangement, as well as providing much of the accompanying explanatory text.

Following his release after a year in prison, King Wen revealed his findings and modifications to his son, the duke of Chou. These were later added to by the duke, who became ruler and founder of the Chou dynasty following the overthrow of Chou Hsin. For this reason, this version of the book is usually referred to as the *Chou-I*, or the *Changes of Chou*.

The final modification and resulting present-day name occurred during 5BC. Kung Fu-Tze (Confucius) studied the *Chou-I* and added further philosophical commentary, so overlaying the Taoist principles with Confucian ideas.

There are two principal methods of reading the *I-Ching*, both of which have their basis in the random generation of binary choices. The traditional method is a complex process involving the manipulation of 50 dried yarrow straws, whereby the resultant patterns denote a certain sequence of hexagrams.

The simple, more commonly used method involves the casting of coins. The side which is uppermost when the coin has fallen relates to the drawing of a yin or yang line, which in turn constitutes the sequence of hexagrams.

Although some controversy surrounds the two systems because of the fact that they give vastly differing distribution patterns for the yin and yang lines, both techniques are respected and widely used as methods of divination and guidance.

The *I-Ching* was first introduced to the West in 1882, when James Legge provided the first English translation. Legge, however, did not approve of the oracular function of the book, and it failed to arouse any significant interest until Jung brought his attention to bear on it.

Jung discovered that consultations with the oracle on a wide range of topics resulted in consistently meaningful and startlingly accurate insights. He subsequently recorded these findings in an introduction to a German translation of the book in 1929. When it was finally translated into English, under the title of *The I-Ching* or *Book of Changes*, in 1949, it was received with great enthusiasm and is still widely used and studied.

Today, the *I-Ching* continues to be held in high esteem all over the world largely as a result of its remarkable powers of prophecy and guidance. Although debate surrounds some of its early history, this has not affected its popularity, and it seems likely that this ancient Eastern oracle will continue to be consulted for the mystical wisdom it contains, for many years to come, by seekers of the truth.

EZEKIEL

The Holy Bible abounds with stirring tales of mankind's deeds, with stories of heroism, war and treachery figuring prominently. Above all, though, it is the prophetic word of God that can be found within its pages. The moral and religious messages of the Bible's many books are delivered for the most part through prophets of the Old Testament such as Ezekiel and Jeremiah.

The Bible contains several main prophetic books, and within each of these is a series of 'Oracles against Foreign Nations'. These highly stylized and poetic sections contain God's predictions about the fate of those nations who commit crimes against humanity and who sin against God. One of the most famous of these indictments can be found in the book of Ezekiel, and it is particularly notable because of the fact that it is dated, and so can be linked to the historical circumstances that surround both its pronouncement and fulfilment.

The oracle against the island city of Tyre, contained within Ezekiel 26, is from 586BC and was a result of the turbulent events in Israel that occurred around the late seventh and early sixth centuries BC. At that time, Babylon, under the awesome auspices of Nebuchadnezzar, was in the process of consolidating and expanding its empire in the Eastern Mediterranean, and was aiming to gain control of Egypt.

Israel, on the other hand, had become weak and vulnerable following the abortive attempts at reform by Josiah in 621BC. This had led to a succession of disorganized and godless leaders, who undermined the nation's commitment to God and made them deaf to the dire warnings of prophets such as Ezekiel and Jeremiah.

Israel was the stepping-stone between Babylon in the east and Egypt in the west, and so invasion was inevitable. It happened in 606BC when Israel became a vassal state of Babylon. Discontent and nationalism brewed as a result and eventually surfaced as a full-scale rebellion against the Babylonian forces. This was quickly quashed, however, and many of the Israeli ringleaders, including Ezekiel, were deported in 598BC.

A few years later, just before the destruction of Jerusalem by the

Babylonians, Ezekiel made his now-famous oracle against Tyre. The city of Tyre, situated very close to the shore of what is now Lebanon, was a significant Phoenician seaport, which linked shipping routes from all over the Mediterranean with land caravans from Arabia, Babylon, Persia and India. Ezekiel predicted that, despite its strong defensive position, Tyre and its land-based 'daughter' villages would be totally destroyed. He prophesied: 'For thus says the Lord GOD: Behold, I will bring upon Tyre from the North Nebuchadnezzar king of Babylon, king of kings, with horses and chariots, and with horsemen and a host of soldiers ... He will slay with the sword your daughters on the mainland.'

These predictions did, in part, subsequently unfold. Historical records, including those written by the Jewish historian Josephus Flavius, relate that Nebuchadnezzar did demolish the mainland parts of the city and lay siege to the island for 13 years. Although this was unsuccessful at the time, Tyre did eventually become a vassal of Babylon as a result of a negotiated settlement.

The overthrow of Jerusalem and the undermining of power in Tyre were viewed as divine retribution by Ezekiel and Jeremiah. In their eyes, the state of Israel had wavered in its faith and failed to serve God, and thus deserved punishment at the hands of Nebuchadnezzar. In turn, it seemed the Babylonians were being rewarded for their punitive actions by allegedly achieving their ambitious invasion of Egypt.

Although many of the specifics of Ezekiel's oracle may not have come to pass exactly as predicted, its message remains abundantly clear, with the factual details taking on a comparatively reduced significance. The fact that Tyre was eventually demolished many years later, in 332BC, by Alexander the Great gives the oracle against Tyre an enduring resonance, and is further evidence of the amazing power of prophecy.

THE ORACLES OF BALAAM

One of the most controversial seers of the Old Testament is Balaam, the barbaric prophet whose name means 'devourer of people'. Although reviled and often attached to the epithet rasha, 'the wicked one', in Rabbinical literature, this mythical figure attained a level of exaltation among the heathens that is sometimes equated with that achieved by Moses among the 'chosen' people.

While some sources proclaim Balaam to be one of the seven heathen prophets, among which his father Job was numbered, others state that his lineage stemmed from Beor, and that he lived in Pethor in Mesopotamia. The prophet is often depicted as being blind in one eye and lame in one foot, with his followers distinguished only by merit of possessing the three morally corrupt qualities of an evil eye, haughtiness and greed.

Balaam started his career as an interpreter of dreams, before becoming a magician and finally a prophet. This gift of prophecy enabled him to predict the exact moment at which God's wrath would occur, and thus his powers could be extremely valuable to the world at large. So great was his reputation as a reliable oracle, that people far and wide asserted 'he whom thou blessest is blessed, and he whom thou cursest is cursed'.

Anxious to secure Balaam's services, Balak – a worshipper of the god Baal and king of Moab, a heathen state embroiled at that time in a bloody battle against the Israelites – sent messengers to summon the infamous soothsayer. Balak, whose name means 'the devastator', had assumed his position of power in Moab following the destruction of the Amorites during the time of Moses.

Balaam, however, having consulted with God and been forbidden to return with Balak's messengers, refused to go. The king, desperate to gain Balaam's assistance in overcoming the Israelites, tried once more, sending further emissaries with more extravagant promises of riches and power.

Balaam was tempted by Balak's enticing offer, and again consulted with God. This time, he was granted permission to return with the messengers, provided that he promised to do only as God commanded. Balaam agreed to this and set out on an ass on the journey to Moab.

According to the story, God was angered by Balaam's motives of greed, and suspected that he would not obey his decree. An angel of the Lord, invisible to the human eye, was sent down, and the ass, which was able to discern the heavenly body, refused to move. At this, Balaam became incensed and proceeded to thrash the animal, but to no avail. The ass was then bestowed with the gift of human speech, reproaching the prophet for his actions. In response, Balaam claimed that, if he had the means, he would kill the ass.

At this point, the angel made himself visible. Balaam bowed down before the divine messenger, confessed his sins and offered to return to his homeland. The angel responded by saying that he could continue his journey, but only if he honoured his promise to the Lord.

Balaam agreed and continued on his journey to Moab. Here, in response to God's instructions, he ordered Balak to offer sacrifices of seven oxen and seven rams on seven altars positioned on high ground overlooking the land of Israel. Balak did so and, accordingly, the two men travelled together to Bamoth-Baal, from where most of Israel could be seen. Here Balaam, obedient to God, delivered the first of the four famous oracles in favour of Israel.

Balak, expecting Balaam to pronounce a curse rather than blessing on his enemy, was annoyed by what he had heard. Nevertheless, he journeyed with the seer to the second of the high places, Mount Pisgah, from where all of the Israeli encampment was visible.

To Balak's increasing vexation, Balaam again spoke in favour of the Israelites, this time praising them even more highly. He compared their might to that of a lion, saying: 'Behold, the people riseth up as a lioness, And as a lion doth he lift himself up; He shall not lie down until he eat of the prey, And drink the blood of the slain.'

Upon hearing this second prediction, Balak begged the prophet to say no more. Balaam, however, maintained that he must fulfil his promise. The pair then journeyed to Mount Peor, which again overlooked the Israeli encampment, and here Balaam delivered his third pronouncement, which predicted the sustained fertility of Israeli soil.

At this point, Balak became enraged, and attempted to dismiss the seer, but was thwarted when Balaam delivered the last and most portentous of his prophecies. In this, he spoke of the rise of the Israelites and their subsequent victory over Moab and the neighbouring states of Edom and the Kenites. Shattered by what he had heard, Balak allowed the seer to his home country, where, at the age of 33, he was stoned, burned, strangled and decapitated for his many wicked deeds.

As a result of what he had been told, Balak ceased his aggression against the Israelites. Despite this, Balaam's prophecy later came true, as Moab fell into the hands of King David of Israel. Not only was Balaam's prediction entirely accurate, but also his remarkable abilities had shown themselves to be so powerful that they had fundamentally influenced the actions of one of the world's most potent leaders.

THE DELPHIC ORACLE

Throughout history, the role of the oracle has figured prominently, as it has in numerous tales of classical mythology. Of all the famous oracles, perhaps the best known and respected was that found at Delphi in Greece.

The oracle at Delphi was at the shrine of Apollo, the Greek god of fine arts and prophecy. Set high on the hillside of Mount Parnassus, it occupied a prominent position, reflecting the esteem in which it was held in Greek culture.

According to legend, Apollo took control of Parnassus when he was a child, by killing Python, a huge dragon snake, in the battle between the gods of the sky and the earth. Apollo then assumed the form of a dolphin (delphis in Greek, from which the shrine derived its name) and journeyed out into the ocean to capture some sailors who were appointed his first high priests.

Apollo delivered his prophecies at Delphi through various prophetesses, or sybils. The sybil, who was always a mature woman who had lived a pure life, would take on the name Pythia upon being appointed, after the python slain by the young Apollo.

When the prophecies were made, Pythia would enter a trance before delivering her predictions in riddles. These were then translated and interpreted by the high priests and then they would be relayed to the waiting supplicants.

Upon arriving at Delphi, these supplicants would have registered and paid a fee to make an appointment. They would then have been required to purify themselves in the Castalian spring, where a bathing trough still exists, and travel up the Sacred Way to the shrine. A sacrificial offering in the form of a sheep or goat would have been made and the entrails examined for omens by priests. When the pilgrims finally reached the sybil, they were allowed in, one at a time, to ask for her predictions.

The Delphic oracle was visited over a period of almost 2,000 years, during which time countless prophecies were delivered on subjects ranging from wars and matters of state to personal affairs, births and deaths. The supplicants came from almost every level of society, a factor that demonstrates the regard in which prophecy was held in the everyday life of those times. The power and influence of the oracle can also be seen in the art and literature of the period. Not only does it figure in Virgil's *Aeneid* and Homer's *Odyssey*, but in Sophocles' story of Oedipus, the oracle predicts to the king and queen of Thebes that their son Oedipus would kill his father and marry his mother. As the dramatic events unfold, the prophecy is fulfilled, evoking questions about fate and morality that are relevant to this day.

THE SANGOMA

Deep in the heart of southern Africa there lives a tradition of healing and divination that is integral to African culture, and is as respected today as it was thousands of years ago. The extraordinary powers of Sangomas, or diviner priests, are a revered alternative to more modern medicine, and their predictions are remarkable in their accuracy. It is estimated that around 200,000 such diviners are practising today, helping more than 84 per cent of the southern African population.

The role of the Sangoma varies and can be divided into two primary categories, although these are by no means rigid. The principal kind of Sangoma is the ancestrally designated diviner who communes with the ancestors, usually by entering a trance, to predict the future. The second type of Sangoma is the herbalist or doctor, who uses traditional methods to cure the sick and has not been called by the ancestors. However, these boundaries are often blurred, as the ancestrally designated diviner is often also a herbalist, consulting the ancestors for guidance on treatments and cures.

Novices (thwasas) begin their training by enduring and surviving an 'initiation illness' (ukuthwasa). This signals that the ancestors, or deceased spirits, have called them to their vocation. The relationship between the novice and the ancestors is forged during the recovery from the illness, and the person assumes a new identity and role in life.

The ancestral link is crucial to the cures and readings that will be made by the Sangoma, as it is believed that the ancestors are the messengers from the higher power, or 'Supreme Being', acting as a link between deity and man. The Sangoma, in turn, provides a mouthpiece for the oracles, and carries out their instructions, in much the same way as the sybils of Roman times delivered prophecies from Apollo.

The deliverance of these oracles fulfils a major social and political function, as the prophecies provide an acceptable arena for debate about issues that may otherwise be taboo or politically dangerous. Predictions are made on subjects ranging from the state of the crops and the weather to personal problems and health issues. Sangomas maintain that illness can be attributed to one of three main causes – the ancestors, witchcraft and 'pollution' (for example, menstruation or miscarriage). Once the root of the problem has been established, the process of healing can begin.

The trance state entered by the diviner is usually central to the process of delivering the oracle. This condition is achieved through a wide variety of

A potential customer examines a Sangoma's wares, which include skulls, bones, dried heads, horns and herbs.

ritualistic methods, including rhythmic drumming, clapping and dancing, the inhalation of herbal medicines (muti) such as snuff, and the burning of incense (indumba). The attire of the Sangoma is also very important, and he will often wear elaborate ostrich feather head-dresses, and tie rattles and beads to his body.

Upon entering the trance, the Sangoma often starts to shake, and his breathing becomes more erratic as the ancestors enter his body. The rhythmic rituals result in hyperstimulation of the body, while the irregular breathing brings on hyperventilation, both of which are said to 'open' the body and mind to allow access to the ancestors. The men then use 'bones' (shells, coins, dice and twigs) as part of the divination ritual, which are thrown on to an impala skin. The position and alignment of the scattered objects are then interpreted, providing the Sangoma with the information required to deliver the oracle or to cure the patient.

The predictions provided by these revered men have become such a normal part of everyday life in these regions that their magical elements tend to be overlooked.

In Western culture, however, the repeated fulfilment of the Sangomas' prophetic pronouncements and incredible cures continues to baffle and astound.

THE BRAHAN SEER

Deep in the mists of the folklore of the Scottish Highlands lies the character of Coinneach Odhar, the 'Brahan Seer'. This enigmatic figure's uncannily accurate powers of prophecy and his eventual trial for witchcraft made him renowned across the land and continue to amaze people to this day.

With little in the way of written evidence about the seer, his actual identity is unclear. Indeed, many of the tales about him have been preserved through oral tradition alone. The only official documents uncovered to date that might relate to this figure are two Commissions of Justice ordering the prosecution for witchcraft of a Keanoch Owir in 1577. However, this date is almost a century earlier than the period described in more traditional tales of the seer's prophesying, and seems unlikely that it relates to the same man.

Local legend identifies the seer as Kenneth Mackenzie, a labourer born in Baile-na-Gille on the Isle of Lewis around 1650. It is said that he lived at Loch Ussie in Ross-shire, where he worked on the Brahan estate, the seat of the Seaforth chieftains, from about 1675. As the last, and most famous, of his fulfilled predictions specifically relates to this family, it seems likely that Mackenzie was the true Brahan Seer (*aka* Coinneach Odhar).

Many of the prophecies made by this figure related to the geographical region in which he lived, where the fulfilment of his predictions can be seen to this day. As many as 150 years prior to the construction of the Caledonian Canal, Coinneach Odhar is reported to have told a listener: 'Strange as it may seem to you this day, the time will come, and it is not far off, when full-rigged ships will be seen sailing eastward and westward by the back of Tomnahurich, near Inverness.' As, at the time of the premonition, the area in question consisted of rolling hills, the listener deemed what he had heard to be so preposterous that from that point on he ceased all contact with the seer.

Another visible example of the seer's prophecies lies in the parish of Petty, where a huge stone once marked the boundary between the estates of Culloden and Moray. In 1799 this colossally heavy stone inexplicably moved some distance into the sea. How or why this occurred remains a mystery, but whatever the cause, the event was specifically foretold by the seer, who predicted: 'The day will come when the stone of Petty, large though it is, and high and dry upon the land as it appears to people this day, will be suddenly found as far advanced into the sea as it now lies away from it inland, and no one will see it removed or be able to account for its sudden and marvellous transportation.'

The seer seems also to have been adept at predicting numerous important events in the history of Scotland, such as his premonitions of the carnage wreaked at the famous battle of Culloden. While walking in the vicinity, he is said to have stated: 'The bleak moore shall, ere many generations have passed away, be stained with the best blood of the Highlands.'

He also accurately foresaw the demise of the clan Mackenzie of Fairburn and its 16th-century Fairburn Tower, which stands high on the ridge between the Orrin and Bonon river valleys. At the time at which the prophecy was made, the Mackenzie clan, presided over by a rich and powerful chieftain, was enjoying success and stability. Nevertheless, the seer made the now-famous claim: 'The day will come when the Mackenzies of Fairburn shall lose their entire possessions; their castle will become uninhabited and a cow shall give birth in the uppermost chamber.'

Unthinkable as this may have seemed at the time, this prophecy has since been fulfilled to the letter. A few generations after the prediction was made, the family lost its power and wealth, and the tower was eventually abandoned, fell into disrepair and was taken over by a farmer, who used the upper floor for storing hay. One day, according to numerous eyewitness reports from 1851, a pregnant cow followed a trail of dropped hay up the precarious staircase to the upper level. Having become stuck, the cow gave birth to her calf right there on the top floor, just as the seer had predicted.

This was not the only fall from greatness accurately predicted by Coinneach Odhar, since he foretold the end of the male line of the Seaforth clan as a result of the premature deaths of all four sons. He also stated that all of the last lord's possessions would be 'inherited by a white-coiffed lassie from the east and she is to kill her sister'.

And so it happened that, upon the death of the last Lord Seaforth, the estate was passed to the eldest remaining daughter, Mary, who was married to Admiral Hood and lived in the East Indies for many years. Upon the admiral's death, Lady Hood returned to her family home wearing a white coif, a traditional Indian mourning garment. Some years later, she lost control of the pony carriage in which she and her sister were travelling, and her sister died.

Coinneach Odhar did not live to see the fulfilment of this prediction, however. Over the years, suspicion about the seer had grown, with his mysterious powers being linked with witchcraft and the dark arts. His fate was sealed when he told Countess Isabella Seaforth, wife of the third Earl of Seaforth, that her husband was having an affair with a Frenchwoman. This news apparently so enraged Isabella that she ordered that he be tried for witchcraft. At the end of his trial the countess had claimed that, in view of his powers of witchcraft, the seer's soul would not be fit for heaven. Upon hearing his sentence, the Brahan Seer had responded with one final prediction. He declared that upon his death, a dove and a raven would meet in the air above his ashes and would instantly alight on them. If, he said, the raven alighted first, then the countess would be correct. However, if the dove should alight first, then his soul would go to heaven, while hers would go to hell. He was found guilty and executed by being pitched into a barrel of burning tar. According to legend, the spectators were astonished when the two birds did appear above his ashes, and awestruck when the dove alighted first.

Many more of the Brahan Seer's predictions have since been proved accurate. Whatever his real identity, it would seem that he really did possess truly mysterious powers of prophecy.

EDGAR CAYCE – THE 'SLEEPING PROPHET'

Edgar Cayce is one of the most famous seers of recent times. During the course of his remarkable life, he gave in excess of 14,000 readings on more than 10,000 different topics, ranging from personal health and emotional issues to the lives of ancient civilizations and natural disasters. The subject of many hundreds of scientific works, and is read by curious minds the world over, in an attempt to unravel the mystery of his incredible powers.

Born in 1877 in rural Hopkinsville, USA, Cayce exhibited early signs of his unusual gifts when he baffled his teachers by absorbing vast amounts of information simply by 'sleeping' on his schoolbooks. Upon leaving school, he became a photographer, but tragedy was to strike him at the age of 21 when he was informed that he was suffering from a rare condition, one that would cause the gradual paralysis of his throat, and subsequent loss of speech.

His miraculous recovery from this devastating illness was to be the first of Cayce's incredible cures. Having entered the same hypnotic sleep as that used to absorb information from his schoolbooks, Cayce was able to divine the cure to his illness. To the astonishment and bafflement of his doctors, his suggestions for treatments were totally successful and he made a full recovery.

Having discovered this amazing gift, Cayce quickly realized that he could use it to help others, and he soon became famous throughout the USA as a great healer. The healing process would begin with his establishing the name of the patient, after which he would enter his hypnotic sleep. He would then search to re-establish contact with the patient, before conducting a long conversation with him or her, prompted by questions from his attendant wife, to divine the symptoms of the illness. His secretary would note down everything he said in order that his response to the medical problem could be recorded.

Having established himself in this way, Cayce began to explore other areas of his hypnotically induced powers. In 1923, while working in a photographic studio in Selma, Alabama, Cayce met a printer, Arthur Lammers, who was to alter the course of his prophesying. Lammers was deeply interested in the subject of metaphysical philosophy, a topic far beyond the possible scope of Cayce's knowledge. Having heard about Cayce's remarkable powers, Lammers was keen to see what answers he might divulge to fundamental metaphysical questions. In this way, he hoped, great areas of uncertainty for mankind, such as the mystery behind the meaning of life, might be clarified.

Cayce agreed to go ahead with this experiment, and produced more than 2,500 'Life' readings over the rest of his life. These 'Life' readings related to information about a person's past life, and were distinct from his 'Physical' readings, which pertained to medical diagnoses and cures. However, these readings induced in Cayce a personal dilemma and crisis of faith. Raised as a devout Protestant, he had difficulty in accepting intuitive information relating to subjects such as reincarnation, which ran contrary to the Christian message.

After a while, though, Cayce managed to reconcile himself with these differences and continued with his work. He subsequently declared that the basis for all the great religions was surprisingly similar, as all the people of the world were united by a collective unconscious. Cayce maintained that it was by tapping into this unconscious, or 'universal memory of nature', that he was able to make such a large number of predictions and readings. However, he was sceptical over suggestions that he was able to gain access to an infinite source of collective wisdom, known as the 'Akashic record'. This was, and still is, a contentious idea, and there was no scientific method by which it could be proved, other than by the fulfilment of his prophecies.

Cayce had a remarkable level of insight into past civilizations such as those of ancient Egypt and Atlantis, and this was a subject of great personal interest to him. One of his claims was that the Sphinx had been built in 10,500BC and that a 'Hall of Records', concealed beneath Atlantis, would be discovered in the late 1990s. Although the latter prediction has not yet come to fruition, many of his other insights are proving to be more accurate.

Cayce's intuitive insights into the nature of our climate seem to be becoming ever more true. Just as he predicted, there has been a marked increase in recent years in the intensity and frequency of natural disasters such as storms, earthquakes and droughts. For example, a great storm has occurred every decade since the 1960s, when, previously, violent weather of this kind used to take place approximately only once every 500 years.

Another of his climatic predictions related to the imminence of polar shift, a switch in the magnetic polarity of the Earth that will have catastrophic consequences for the planet. Scientists today believe that Cayce's prognostications may prove to be correct, and that just such a devastating switch could occur.

Similarly, Cayce's prediction of the destruction and submergence of certain parts of the USA is also proving a very real concern among both meteorologists and scientists. Recent information has revealed that one flank of the Cumbre Vieja volcano on the island of La Palma, in the Canaries, is unstable and could plunge into the ocean during the next eruption of the volcano.

This would mean that almost 20km^3 (4.8 miles^3)of rock, weighing 500 billion tonnes, could fall into the water to a depth of more than 6km (3.7 miles) . The effect of this would be the creation of an undersea wave more than 600m (1,970ft) high, which within five minutes would rise to the surface to form a huge tsunami, more than 1.5km (almost a mile) high. This would then disperse in all directions to form a 100m (328ft) wave travelling at the speed of a jet aircraft, which may have the capacity to devastate the east coast of the United States, the Caribbean and Brazil. The events of 26 December 2004 make this prediction even more alarming.

With global warming already evident, and modern technology confirming Cayce's predictions of polar shift and global devastation, it seems that this relatively modern seer was in possession of some truly remarkable gifts. How or why he obtained these incredible intuitive powers, however, remains a mystery that may never be solved.

TITANIC PREDICTIONS

The sinking of RMS *Titanic* is such a dramatic story that it is still being told today, all over the world. Most people are aware of the main causes of the tragedy – the freak iceberg and the shortage of lifeboats – but very few realize that, 14 years prior to the accident, a book was published that set out almost the exact details of the entire incident.

The Wreck of the Titan, or *Futility*, written by a little known author, Morgan Robertson, appeared in print in 1898. Receiving little attention, the book tells the story of a 70,000-tonne 'unsinkable' ocean liner named the SS *Titan*, which hit an iceberg on its fourth voyage across the Atlantic. The ship, bearing a number of wealthy and powerful dignitaries, was equipped with fewer than half the necessary lifeboats, and consequently more than

The GREATEST WRECK in HISTORY
THE LOSS OF THE WHITE STAR TITANIC
THE LARGEST SHIP IN THE WORLD, WHICH SANK ON ITS MAIDEN VOYAGE, WITH A LOSS OF 1635 LIVES

An article from 1912, depicting lifeboats being lowered after RMS Titanic *struck an iceberg.*

two-thirds of the 2,500 passengers on board perished in icy waters when the liner sank.

The parallels with the true story of the RMS *Titanic* are immediately apparent. Moreover, there are further, uncanny, similarities between the fictitious and real vessels, in details such as the weight of the ship, the nationality of the principal shareholders involved, the time of the impact and the number of lifeboats on board.

Incredibly, this was not the only time that a prediction was made about the fate of the *Titanic*. A few years prior to the publication of *The Wreck of the Titan*, a similar story had appeared in a newspaper article. A prophetic note by the editor at the end of the piece warned that 'this is exactly what might take place, and what will take place, if liners are sent to sea short of boats'.

In a chilling irony, this editor was one of the very passengers who perished when the RMS *Titanic* sank beneath the waves 20 years later. Could this really be merely a cruel twist of fate, or was some higher power at work?

THE UNKNOWN PROPHET

Early in the First World War came the discovery of a man who was remarkable for his powers of prophecy, making a series of astoundingly accurate predictions about events that would occur during, and after, both World Wars. Very little is known about this individual, other than that he was French, and he appeared to be a holy man. Whoever he was, his unique gifts have baffled experts for many decades.

In 1914, two German soldiers captured a lone Frenchman in the Alsace region of France. They imprisoned and questioned him, and it was during this interrogation that the extraordinary predictions were made. One of the soldiers, Andreas Rill, was so amazed by what he had heard that he wrote detailed accounts of the incident in letters to his family.

The unknown prophet predicted not only that the war was going to last for five years, but also that Germany would lose. There would then be a revolution, followed by a period of great prosperity in which, amazingly, money would be flung out of windows to lie untouched on the ground.

He said that, during this period, an antichrist would be born, who would begin a nine-year reign of tyranny in 1932, passing new legislation and secretly impoverishing the people of Germany. Preparations for a second war, that would last three years, would commence in 1939, and this time Italy would be allied to Germany, rather than fighting against it as it had in the previous conflict. Despite this, however, Germany would again lose. The German people would then rise up against the tyrant and his followers, and 'the man and his sign would disappear'. In a year containing the numerals '4' and '5', Germany would be surrounded by its enemies and destroyed.

History proved the amazing veracity of these predictions. The First World War, in which Italy fought against Germany, did last five years, and Germany did lose. This was followed by inflation in which the German currency became so devalued as to be worthless.

Adolf Hitler's rise to power began during the 1920s, and in 1933 the National Socialist German Workers' (Nazi) Party commenced its oppressive reign, with Hitler at the helm, despite the fact that they had only 37 per cent of the vote. The Nazis then passed the Enabling Act, allowing Hitler to pass any new law he so desired, thus effectively signalling the demise of democracy and the dawn of dictatorship.

Preparations for the start of what was to be the Second World War began, as predicted, in 1939 when Germany invaded Poland. This conflict lasted until 1945, when the Germans were surrounded and forced to surrender. Hitler committed suicide and the arrival of the Allies resulted in the end of the reign of the Nazi Party.

Rill was amazed to watch history unfold in line with the prophet's statements and, as time went by, the letters to his family became famous for their contents. Indeed, at one point they almost resulted in Rill's internment in a concentration camp due to their predictions about the imminent rise of a dictator.

The letters then lay dormant during the turbulent years of the Second World War, surfacing only briefly in 1950 when they appeared in a mission journal, published by a Father Frumentius Renner. This publication passed almost unnoticed and no attempts were made to check the authenticity of

The letters then arrived at the Freiburg Institute for Border Areas of Psychology and Mental Hygiene. Here, the accuracy of their contents provoked such suspicion that forgery was suspected and, accordingly, the documents were subjected to extensive testing and scrutiny by a team of expert criminologists. Following these investigations, it was declared that the letters were the genuine documents that Rill had sent home to his family back in 1914.

It was then decided to try to locate the mysterious seer, not an easy task as Rill had died. Professors Hans Bender and Elber Gruber traced Rill's movements in an effort to establish the locality in which the man had been arrested. They conducted interviews with Rill's family, learning from his son that the visionary had apparently been a rich man who had given his wealth away in order to join a holy order. His son also remembered that his father had himself attempted to locate the nameless prophet in 1918, while posted in the town of Colmar. Upon arriving at the nearby monastery in Sogolsheim, he was reportedly told that the man had died.

The results of these interviews and their own painstaking detective work led the two professors to believe that this monastery had indeed been the last residence of the prophet.

After consulting monastery records, they established that he may have been Frater Laicus Tertiarius, who had died in 1917, not long before Rill's visit. This man seems to have stayed at the monastery as a guest rather than as a monk, which supports the theory that he had indeed been a rich man and consequently would have been barred from joining the brotherhood.

While it is true that this prophet did make some predictions that were not eventually realized, this may have been the fault of inaccurate recollection of the details by Rill, or even linguistic errors on the part of the Frenchman while speaking German.

Overall, the accuracy of his predictions is truly astonishing, especially in view of the fact that the prophet could have had no knowledge about events that would only take place decades after his death.

How this anonymous seer achieved his prophetic visions is a mystery, and can only be attributed to the incredible powers of foresight.

THE HITLER HOROSCOPES

Countless history books have recorded, analysed and discussed the events that occurred before, during and after the Second World War, but, of these, few mention the significant part that astrology and prophecy played in determining the course of history. It is now known that both Stalin and Hitler frequently consulted seers and mind readers, even though, officially, they had forbidden the employment of such mysterious powers. In Nazi Germany, in particular, occultists suffered harassment and persecution, in common with all other minority groups.

Prior to the outbreak of war, a prophet and astrologer, Karl Ernst Krafft, was gaining great respect in Germany among his contemporaries. Born in Basle in 1900, Krafft was highly numerate, especially in the field of statistics, and was also passionate about astrology. However, it was the publication of his book, *Traits of Astro-Biology*, that was to raise him to such an extent in the estimation of fellow prophets and occultists. In this work, Krafft expounded his theory on predicting the future, which he termed 'typoscomy'. Essentially, this maintained that a person's destiny could be predicted on the basis of his or her personality.

When the war commenced, Krafft's privileged position was placed in peril. However, his life changed dramatically when a remarkably accurate prediction about Hitler brought him face to face with leading members of the Führer's command. Krafft foresaw that Hitler's life would be in peril at some point between 7 and 10 November 1939. In fact, he was so sure of this that on 2 November of that year he wrote to Dr Heinrich Fesel, a close acquaintance of Himmler, warning him of Hitler's impending fate. Fesel, not wanting to be associated with the prophet, filed the letter away without mentioning it to Himmler. On 8 November a bomb exploded in the Munich beer hall just 27 minutes after Hitler had left the building. When the story became known, Fesel immediately supposed that Krafft must have been involved in the plot to kill the Führer, and so gave the letter to Hitler's right-hand man, Rudolf Hess.

Krafft was immediately arrested by the Gestapo, but they found him innocent of conspiring to kill Hitler. At this point, word of Krafft's remarkable powers reached the ears of Joseph Goebbels, head of the Ministry for Propaganda, who had recently become fascinated with the works of Nostradamus. Goebbels ordered that Krafft be employed to decipher Nostradamus' complex quatrains and extract any references which could be inferred as good omens for the Third Reich and which could be used for propaganda purposes.

Then, in 1940, Krafft was called to give a horoscope reading for Hitler. In this, he advised that a planned attack on the USSR be postponed until a later date. In spite of the fact that he had not actually met Krafft personally, Hitler followed his recommendation and waited until the following June before launching Operation Barbarossa.

The success of the attack on the USSR in the early days of the offensive seemed to prove Krafft's prediction to be correct, although this ultimately proved unsustained.

Krafft then insisted that it was imperative that Germany secured victory by 1943 at the latest, or else the war would be lost. Although history was to reveal the accuracy of this prophecy, the result for Krafft was that he was imprisoned. Hitler was enraged by his prediction, and cited it as the reason for the sudden defection of Hess in 1941. As a result, all occultists and astrologers were rounded up and put in prison.

Upon his release in 1942, Krafft was ordered to study the horoscopes of Allied leaders in order to provide his leaders with vital information about the enemy. Among his many readings was his divination that Montgomery would prove a stronger enemy than Rommel, an insight which proved to be correct.

His final, accurate, premonition – that a bomb would destroy the propaganda ministry in Berlin – resulted in Krafft being tried for treason.

After languishing in prison for several years, he eventually contracted typhus and died in 1945.

The remarkable accuracy with which Krafft made his predictions seems undoubted proof of his oracular powers. In fact, Krafft's abilities so impressed the Allies that they attempted to find a seer of comparable skill to assist them in much the same way as Krafft had helped the Nazis. The fact that they were unable to do so demonstrates how rare and precious Krafft's talent really was.

GORDON SCALLION

Gordon Scallion is one of the most popular seers of modern times, enjoying particular acclaim in the USA for his incredible powers of prophecy. Because of these gifts he has become the author of numerous books, as well as a teacher of consciousness studies, and he has found special fame over the years through his many television appearances.

In common with many prophets, he is said to have obtained his special talents while being struck down by illness. In 1979, having been rendered temporarily dumb following a period of sickness, Scallion is said to have witnessed the unfolding of future events on a type of inner television screen. At this time a mysterious 'shining lady' had apparently appeared before him, informing him of his impending gift.

Having recovered from his illness and regained the power of speech, the visions and predictions continued. He found that, in common with Edgar Cayce before him, he was able to prescribe cures for the infirm and disabled, even when there was a considerable distance between him and the patient. At this time, Scallion also worked as a lecturer, and founded the Matrix Institute, where records of his visions are stored to this day.

After some years spent working as a healer, Scallion noticed that his talent seemed to be shifting, and he found himself able to predict the changing state of the Earth. One powerful vision involved the physical body of the Earth, which appeared to him to be in some distress. It seemed that a bulge had formed in the Earth's core, which was altering its mass. Ultimately, Scallion maintained, this would result in a massive upheaval at the Earth's crust, causing dramatic changes to the position and size of the continents.

Scallion reported these predictions in his newsletter, 'The Earth Changes', and the continental shifts are also illustrated on a new map of the world. He warned that these disruptions at the Earth's crust will lead to huge earthquakes, with the eventual submergence under the sea of large tracts of land. He also envisioned polar shift and the emergence of new land masses.

Of all his numerous predictions, however, perhaps none was more impressive than his foreseeing of Hurricane Andrew in August 1992. The details of his prophecy were remarkably accurate, especially over matters such as the range of dates on which the hurricane might strike, the wind velocity, the path of the storm and the extent of the damage caused.

In his newsletter, he also accurately predicted the 1984 Mexico City earthquake, the 1988 election of President Bush, the 1987 stock market crash and a series of major earthquakes and volcanic disturbances both in California and Japan.

Further endorsement of his accuracy seems to have been given more recently by the scientific press, which has revealed its concerns about the possibility of impending polar shift and the potential occurrence of a mega tsunami. On 26 December 2004 the world witnessed the powerfully destructive forces that Scallion predicted. This event, combined with the increasing occurrence of violent weather and devastating earthquakes, would seem to be undeniable proof that Scallion's predictions are coming true.

MYSTERIOUS MONUMENTS

The power of many ancient monuments is undeniable. They were built to immortalize a set of beliefs, and the scale of their construction shows the effort and dedication that went into their making.

Some of these ancient edifices are enigmas, raising more questions than they answer and fuelling debate through the ages. Why were they built just there? Why were such rare and hard-to-come-by materials used? Perhaps one day, the answers will be discovered, but until then, these ancient monuments serve as tangible reminders of the mysteries of the ancient world.

BAALBECK

Temples have stood at Baalbeck, in Lebanon, for thousands of years, enduring the rule of numerous civilizations and the worship of many changing gods. They have been altered, but never destroyed, because of their incredible beauty and grandeur. In fact, it is the sheer scale of the temples that has provoked such intrigue and wonder, with archaeologists the world over mystified as to how such impressive structures could have been built so long ago.

Baalbeck was originally a Phoenician settlement which became successively Greek, Roman, Byzantine and then Arab, through conquest. The Greeks occupied the town in 331BC, renaming it Heliopolis (city of the sun). Located on principal trading routes, the city flourished and became a large religious centre.

Wherever structures have survived this long, they have usually been built from stone with the express intention of permanence, and Baalbeck is no exception. In fact, this structure contains the largest cut blocks of stone in the world. Some of these are so large, and quarried from so far away, that experts are mystified not only as to how they were transported to the site, but also how the temple was ever built.

The reason for the inconceivable vastness of the stones was Phoenician tradition, which dictated that the podium for the temple must consist of no more than three layers of stone. When a large extension to the temple site was suggested, the ancient architects realized that they were going to have to work on a scale not previously imagined.

Undeterred by the scale of their task, they commissioned the carving of what were in effect colossal building bricks, hewn from solid rock. Several of these are to be found on the western side of the podium, in the area named the 'Trilithon', after the three largest blocks. These stones are around 20m long, 4.5m high and 3.6m deep 66ft x 15ft x 12ft), and each is estimated to weigh around 800 tonnes. By way of comparison, these stones are four or five times larger than those at Stonehenge, and approximately 300 times heavier than those used to build the Egyptian pyramids.

Amazingly, the largest of the stones was even heavier than this. At more than 1,000 tonnes, the size and weight of 'the stone of the pregnant woman' would test the greatest cranes in existence in the world today. However, this stone still remains in its quarry, as building work ceased before it ever came to be used.

Aside from the fact that the huge blocks of stone were transported more than a kilometre from their quarry and then raised more than 7m (23ft) into their final positions, there is yet another mystery attached to them. The craftsmanship shown in the construction is of such a high standard, with the stones arranged in such a precise fashion, without the use of mortar, that it is impossible to wedge even the slightest object between them.

The scale of Baalbeck has fired people's imaginations to such an extent that each successive culture to occupy the site has linked the Trilithon with some kind of popular myth, be it giants, biblical figures or even the intervention of extra-terrestrials.

Whatever the explanation for the construction of this vast monument, it looks likely that Baalbeck will continue to draw countless visitors to the site in the future.

No doubt these people, like thousands before them, will marvel at the beauty of this remarkable ancient monument, that suggests so much about the possibilities of human achievement.

NEWGRANGE

The Megalithic tombs of Newgrange, in Ireland, are more than 5,000 years old, so they pre-date the pyramids of Egypt, and even the arrival of the Celts in Ireland. As is often the case with such ancient monuments, very little remains today to give a clue as to the greater purpose behind their construction and this fine Stone Age necropolis is a source of speculation and intrigue all over the world.

Located near the banks of the river Boyne, to the east of Slane, the Newgrange tombs are known in the native tongue as Bru Na Boinne.

According to pagan lore, Newgrange was the dwelling of Aengus, the powerful god of love. The site is also associated with the mystical race of the goddess Danu, also known as the Tuatha De Dannan. According to local superstition, these nature-loving pagans have left something of their spirit in the landscape and it is thought that Cuchulain, the legendary hero of the Celtic warriors, was conceived at Newgrange.

The Newgrange tomb is said to be the burial place of the high kings of Tara. The ash remains of these rulers would have been contained in large bowls in each of the three recesses of the burial chamber. Although this chamber has been described as cruciform in shape, given the fact that the tomb pre-dates the birth of Christ by around 3,200 years, it is more likely that this layout reflects the clover form that is so prevalent in ancient Irish artworks.

The builders of these tombs demonstrated considerable devotion to their construction. First, they made use of materials that were not readily available – the quartz must have been quarried and transported from the Wicklow Mountains, a considerable distance from Newgrange. Second, the builders were involved in a huge project – it has been estimated that the construction of the monument would have taken a workforce of 300 men more than 20 years to complete.

In common with the people of other ancient cultures, the lives of the Newgrange community would have been closely regulated by the natural rhythms and cycles of the Earth, with the summer and winter solstices assuming great importance. At Newgrange, at the winter solstice, the dawn sun shines through a 'roof-box', down a short, straight passage and into the heart of the burial chamber, illuminating intricate carvings that are believed to represent the sun and the moon.

Intriguingly, similar effects can be found at Stonehenge, in the pyramids of the Maya and Aztec, and in King Khufu's pyramid in Egypt, where a curious shaft of light enters the tomb at the time of the solstice.

It is unclear whether this shaft may have been intended to allow the king's soul to ascend to the heavens.

Did these cultures have a common spiritual identity, or is there simply something innate in human nature that discovered great profundity in the movement of the stars and the cycles of the planet? These ancient farming communities possessed a knowledge and understanding way ahead of their time. It is impossible not to marvel at the skill that enabled these people to make the precise calculations necessary in order to align the passages of the tombs with the light thrown out by the stars or the sun.

YONAGUNI

In 1985, a discovery was made in Japan that still baffles the scientific community today. A Japanese dive tour operator, Kihachiro Aratake, strayed from his regular area into the waters off Yonaguni Island, near Okinawa. About 30m (100ft) beneath the surface, he found a strange formation which, on further examination, appeared to be a man-made pyramid.

Ever since this date, the Yonaguni finding has been a source of immense controversy. Experts are unable to agree upon whether it is actually a man-made structure at all, or simply a remarkable natural formation. If it can be confirmed to be man-made, it will undoubtedly revolutionize the way in which the history of our own species is viewed.

Scientists agree that this area of coastline became submerged by the rising oceans at least 10,000 years ago. Following the end of the last Ice Age, there was a huge global thaw that altered the world immeasurably and, over time, sea levels are believed to have risen by up to 30m. Any civilization in place at that time would have been destroyed, engulfed by the rising waters, with all traces of it remaining hidden to this day.

Furthermore, it is known that human civilizations have thrived on coastlines for thousands of years, because the sea is not only an excellent source of food, but also facilitates important activities such as trading and transport. Yonaguni would, therefore, have been a likely location for a settlement to arise. Such a civilization would, however, have pre-dated all known cultures by thousands of years, since the oldest known city is believed to be Sumeria in Mesopotamia, which dates back to around 5,000 years ago. To double the accepted timescale of human development is to take a drastic leap. This, however, is not impossible, especially if there is real evidence to support it, as Yonaguni might prove to be.

Perplexing scientists still further is the fact that similarities have been noted between the architecture that appears to exist at Yonaguni and that which can be found above the sea on the coast of Peru.

Yet even the oldest of these Peruvian structures, built by the Moche people, are at the most 2,000 years old, leaving an inexplicable gap of many millennia.

Further controversy has arisen over the actual appearance of the Yonaguni structure. Underwater photographs of the site appear to show the presence of ramps, terraces and steps. While American geologists argue that these are nothing more than natural formations, Japanese scientists have claimed that tool markings can be found along the structure, suggesting that it might have been tampered with.

One person, however, has seemingly taken both sides of the argument, asserting that the site is both natural and man-made. Dr Robert M. Schoch, a geologist who made frequent dives to the site, actually suggested that the majority of the structure was indeed a natural formation, but one that had been chosen and modified by humans, in a process known as 'terra-forming'. The discovery of what appeared to be a small staircase on the site was prime evidence of such modification.

The discovery of structures beneath the sea always generates intrigue and excitement, with people proclaiming that the lost city of Atlantis has been uncovered. However, the location of Yonaguni means that it is unlikely to have been Atlantis. Rather, it would seem to have closer parallels to the lost continents of Mu or Lemuria, as both were said to exist in the region of Asia, spanning the Pacific and Indian oceans respectively.

Although the comparatively modern science of tectonics has largely discredited the notion that there were ever 'lost continents', many believe that they did, in fact, exist. Lemuria and Mu are supposed to have been destroyed by immense natural disasters that engulfed the continents. It is not impossible that ancient myths telling of the demise of whole civilizations have become altered and enhanced over time to encompass the destruction of entire continents. In this respect it could actually be possible that the end of the Yonaguni culture could have been mythologized or exaggerated into a story such as that surrounding Lemuria.

In drawing these parallels between Yonaguni and the mythical continents, the experts involved are hoping to advance the theory that there is a great lost culture of the Pacific. Tantalizing glimpses of such a culture are offered by the mysterious stone heads of Easter Island or the oral traditions of the Polynesian islands. Apparent similarities between Yonaguni and stone constructions on Hawaii and Tonga suggest a cultural bridge from prehistoric Japan to the coast of South America.

This theory also attempts to explain the similarities between many different cultures of the world, a large number of which shared a belief in astronomy and adopted the pyramid as a favoured type of construction. Some theorists, such as Graham Hancock, believe that this serves as evidence of an ancient seafaring culture that spread its wisdom around the globe. It is certain, however, that further proof will be required before the sceptical world of archaeology accepts such a drastic reinterpretation of man's early history.

Perhaps, if the site around the pyramid is explored further, this evidence might be found after all. Or, if not, it is possible that proof could be located at other formations that have been discovered on the sea bed close to the Japanese islands of Kerama and Chatan, and in the Straits of Taiwan. Now that technology is able to reveal more and more about global changes as a result of the Ice Age, it seems likely that further discoveries of this kind will be made in shallow coastal shelves around the world.

This offers us the exciting prospect of possible answers as to the nature of the origins of human civilization, but as always, each discovery is likely to raise further questions. Why, for example, has the pyramid been so evident in disparate cultures at different times of mankind's history? The answer to this question looks set to remain one of the greatest mysteries of the ancient world.

RELIGIOUS PHENOMENA

In Christianity the most commonly reported apparition is that of the Virgin Mary. The Hindu religion contains numerous reports of statues that appear to drink milk. Muslims have identified frequent representations of Allah within the natural world. Other creeds have reported weeping statues. For every person who believes implicitly in the validity of religious miracles and phenomena, there will be someone who will just as vehemently reject the notion.

What these people share, however, is a fundamental inability to prove their beliefs one way or the other.

SHAMANISM

The mystical figure of the shaman has existed in human culture for thousands of years on almost every continent of the world, and yet the nature of shamanic powers remains largely unexplained. Widely dismissed by the scientific community, the fact remains that shamanism has played a powerful role in both healing and divination, and continues to do so today in some remote parts of the world such as the Amazonian rainforests and in tribal areas of Mongolia.

Although the word 'shaman' is derived from the Tungus language of Siberian Russia, the practice of shamanism extends far across the globe. Separate disciplines can be classified as Turkic, Mongolian, Manchu-Tunguz, Korean, Japanese, Finno-Ugrian, American-Indian, Celtic and African, all of which are modelled on the same basic principles.

Now perceived as something of a witch doctor, the shaman enjoyed a role in ancient society as a healer and counsellor, and was in many ways a kind of primitive psychotherapist. People would consult the shaman to be healed of their physical, mental or emotional ailments, or to discover secrets from the future or the past. The shaman was able to perform these roles by acting as a psychic bridge between this world and the next.

Central to the principle of shamanism is the concept of 'soul flight'. Any medicine man or woman whose practice revolved around the flight of the soul was classed as a shaman. These people believed that a portion of the human soul could readily leave the body – for example, when in a dream state. In order to help others, the shaman first had to set about releasing his own soul, in the process achieving what has been described as 'a state of ecstasy'.

This state of altered consciousness could be brought about by several means,often combined, such as repetitive chanting, drumming and meditation. Shamans had an extensive knowledge of nature, particularly botany and would also use hallucinogenic plants or fungi, such as mushrooms, to induce their dream state. These substances were often poisonous, so the shaman was at risk of coma, collapse or even death.

Once in this trance-like condition, the shaman would then be able to commune with the hidden spirit world. Believing that knowledge is contained in nature itself, he would consult the rocks, trees and soil, and would also speak with the powerful animal spirits to divine useful wisdom.

This belief in power animals was integral to shamanic practice. In a concept that is similar to that of a guardian angel, power animals are spiritual guardians that watch over the souls of all people. The shaman believed that each person has their own spirit animal, the characteristics of which manifest themselves in personal attributes. For instance, a bear spirit lends a person bear wisdom, which will be recognizable from his or her behaviour.

Having consulted the land or animal spirits, the shaman would then be able to help people with a particular problem or cure them of their ailments. If a man required advice on a difficult decision, the shaman could consult with his personal animal spirits. If there was a blight on the land, or a disease, the shaman would be asked to commune with the land to find the reason and the cure. In the case of some illnesses, such as depression or coma, the shaman would attribute this to the fact that a portion of that person's soul had become lost. It would be the shaman's task to enter the spirit world and guide the soul back safely.

The notion of 'soul flight', so fundamental to shamanism, is not an uncommon one. For example, the idea that it is wrong to wake a sleepwalker dates back to the pagan belief that their soul has become separated from their body and, if the sleepwalker is woken prematurely, that soul will be unable to locate its rightful owner in order to return. Interestingly, accounts of near-death, or out-of-body experiences are often described in terms of the soul leaving the body. Individuals who have had such experiences frequently relate their feelings of being divorced from their bodies, before being eventually reunited with them once the episode is over.

When the shaman's communications with the spirit world have ceased and he has awoken from his trance-like condition, he shares the experience with his tribe through song, dance and storytelling. If he has eaten hallucinogenic mushrooms, the shaman might sometimes decide to involve others in their experience in a rather unusual way. As the active ingredient of this potent fungus can not be broken down by the human body, it would be passed in his urine, which the shaman dilutes and passes to other members of the tribe. In this way, everyone can experience a portion of the 'ecstasy' felt by the shaman.

Some believe that the role of the shaman can be compared to that of the faith healer, with the patients believing so utterly in the mystical power of the shaman to cure them that they would, in effect, make themselves better – in other words, a kind of self-hypnosis would take place. Others maintain, however, that maybe it is time to re-assess the power of our ancestral knowledge in light of the incredible success of the shaman over thousands of years. Surely, they argue, this is based on something more solid than mere psychosomatic superstition?

It has been suggested that the shaman may have had some kind of psychic link with the earth that is unknown to the modern world. Shamanic practices were prevalent in hunter-gatherer societies, among people who lived close to the natural order, and whose lives were regulated by the natural rhythms of the seasons.

With the advent of agriculture, man became able to control certain aspects of nature, such as the crops, and once this happened there was less fear and superstition concerning the ultimate power of nature. It could be that, in breaking our link with nature, we have lost a vital store of knowledge that was well known to the shaman, wherever in the world he happened to be.

From whatever source the shaman derived their remarkable gifts, it is true to say that there are many today who believe strongly in their psychic abilities, and in the power manifest in the spirits of the natural world.

If we cast our eyes back to the past, rather than fixing them on the future, we may discover that our ancestors were not really that primitive after all.

APPARITIONS OF THE VIRGIN MARY

Although religious visions have been witnessed by many people over hundreds of years, a few of these apparitions have been actively endorsed by the Church, or had the power to make sceptics think twice.

In 1968, in Zeitun, Egypt, more than one million people were stunned to witness an apparition of the Virgin Mary hovering above the town's church. The visitation was visible for varying durations of time, sometimes even for several hours at once, and continued to happen for almost a year.

The actual form of the apparition varied from night to night, reducing markedly the chances that the vision could have been the result of some kind of deception. On some evenings, the full figure of the Virgin Mary would be visible, whereas at other times only her head could be seen. On several occasions, she would be accompanied by a number of birds, which were taken to be doves of peace. These were seen to move around and were controversially photographed flying in the formation of a cross – although close inspection of the photographs has proved that they were live birds rather than part of the apparition. A number of observers sent from the Egyptian Coptic Church also claimed to witness plumes of fragrant purple smoke coming from the church during the apparitions.

Word spread about the remarkable occurrence and pilgrimages were made from miles around. Large numbers of miraculous healings were reported, such as cripples finding that they could walk and the blind regaining their sight. Of all the miracles achieved by the apparition, however, perhaps the greatest of these was the sense of common destiny that it fostered among many peoples of disparate religions. In a region such as Egypt, where conflict has existed between different creeds for hundreds of years, it was amazing in itself for all people to agree that what they were seeing with their own eyes seemed indeed to be a religious miracle, and could not be explained without God. Muslims who saw the vision chanted passages from the Koran, such as: 'Mary, God has chosen thee. And purified thee; He has chosen thee. Above all women.' If there were

Another visionary: Crowds watch 14-year-old Marie-Bernarde Soubirous (later to become St Bernadette) experience one of her 18 visions of the Virgin Mary in the grotto of Massabielle in Lourdes in France.

any celestial message implicit in the apparition, it was one of unity and tolerance, as was displayed before the vision.

The apparitions attracted a high level of public attention, and were not only photographed, but also broadcast on television. The fact that there were so many witnesses, combined with the high level of public acceptance of the phenomenon, served only to increase the validity of the apparition. The Egyptian president himself, Gamel Abdul Nasser, a lifelong Marxist with nothing to gain by acknowledging the event, witnessed and verified the apparition.

The authorities, however, believed that the vision was the result of an elaborate hoax. Accordingly, the police carried out an exhaustive search over a 25km (15 miles) radius for any evidence of foul play, but were unable to find anything.

Everyone was asking one question – was the apparition genuine and, if so, what was its significance? Opinions on a subject such as this will always be staunchly divided. There is always the possibility that the vision was the result of unscrupulous activities and that the whole event was staged for some ulterior motive.

Alternatively, there are people who claim to have been cured of lifelong afflictions by coming into the vicinity of the beatific presence, although this could perhaps be attributed to the strength of their beliefs rather than to divine intervention.

It is unlikely that the world will ever know the answer to the question of the vision's validity, leaving it a resounding mystery to all.

TALKING IN TONGUES

The practice of 'talking in tongues' (glossolalia) has existed in many forms in different cultures and religions all over the world. Over the last century it has become well known to Christianity, especially within the Pentecostal Church movement. Although its validity has been questioned by many within mainstream religion, the practice of glossolalia nevertheless has many adherents.

Essentially, 'talking in tongues' describes the uttering of words and sounds that are unintelligible to all except those gifted with the power of translation. Christian Pentecostalists believe that the sounds made are actually a manifestation of the Holy Spirit entering the mind and body of the faithful, and communing with the world. Similar to glossolalia is xenolalia, the name given to speaking in a language that is foreign to the speaker, and yet is known and understood by others.

Many references to both types of phenomena, occurring separately or even together, can be found within the pages of the Holy Bible, especially in the descriptions of the Day of Pentecost, from which the Pentecostal Church derives its name. The instance is described by Luke: 'the faithful talking in tongues were taken by the bystanders for being drunken men, but intoxicated men do not talk in languages of which they are normally ignorant'.

The Pentecostal movement appears to have been born in around 1900 following an episode of 'talking in tongues' and subsequent interpretation at the church of a preacher named Charles Fox Parham. Following one of Parham's sermons, a member of the church, Agnes Ozman, stunned listeners with a revelatory outburst, which was in essence an example of spontaneous glossolalia. Parham declared that the utterance was a 'Pentecostal blessing', and this branch of the Church has been in existence ever since.

Certain elements of 'talking in tongues' seem related to the practice of hypnosis and the religious or supernatural belief in possession. Indeed, adherents within the Pentecostal Church believe that those who speak in this way are being possessed by the Holy Spirit. Before the utterances are made, a trance-like state of ecstasy occurs, this higher state of consciousness being common in many other rites and rituals that attempt to form connections with other worlds.

At séances, for example, mediums usually need to enter a trance before they can contact the spirits of the deceased. Similarly, a shaman needs to go into a state of ecstasy before he is able to commune with his spirit guides. It

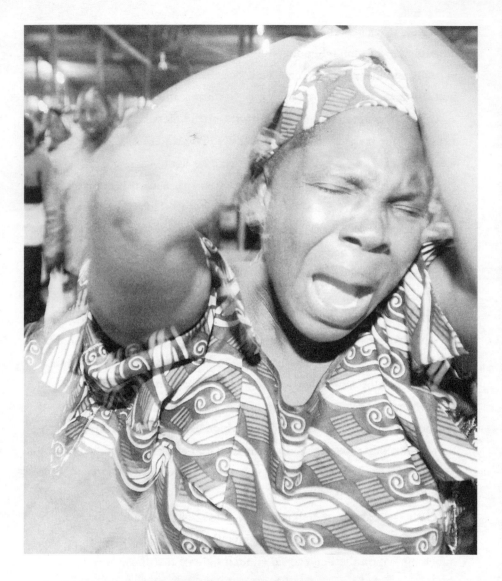

A woman possessed by a spirit at a Pentecostal service in Nigeria.

seems that certain individuals really do have the ability to experience some form of communication with the spirit world when they are in such a state of trance. The difference in this case is that, with glossolalia, another party is required to actually interpret the language as it is heard.

While the practice of 'talking in tongues' has many believers around the world, it has nevertheless aroused much doubt and suspicion. Many of the instances of glossolalia that have been judged as blessings could just as easily, in other religions, have been deemed to be curses, or evidence of demonic possession.

Perhaps, however, it is neither possession nor blessing, but is in reality something more basic. It could be that the utterings are no more than the result of the trance-like state itself, very similar to the vague mutterings of a person who is fast asleep. After all, the state of trance is similar to that of sleep, in many ways. The strange outbursts of glossolalia could be little more than a primal mental process at work.

There are many who would argue, though, that the mystery lies not in how the utterances are produced, but in how their meaning comes to be deciphered.

In the practice of xenolalia, although the speaker has no knowledge of the language in which he is speaking, at least his words are intelligible to those listening.

In glossolalia, however, there is no real possibility of proving what is being said and so the potential for an unscrupulous preacher to deceive a congregation in this way should not be overlooked. This is probably the main reason why the practice of 'talking in tongues' continues to be viewed with suspicion by a large part of the Church.

Others would argue, though, that this practice is a prime example of an alternative method of communication about which the world still has much to learn. It looks as if the mystery will continue.

MAITREYA AND THE CRYSTAL TEARS

In 1996 an incredible event took place that stunned the world, for it defied any kind of medical explanation. As if this were not remarkable enough in itself, it was also accompanied by numerous religious visions of the mystical figure of Maitreya, a teacher and saviour of mankind.

The strange events started in March of that year, when a 12-year-old

Lebanese girl, Hasnah Mohamed Meselmani, was amazed to discover that solid crystals of glass were emerging from her eyes several times a day. These crystals were sharp enough to cut paper, and yet their appearance did not seem to be causing her any pain. The process continued over a period of eight months, during which time she produced an average of seven crystals a day.

Shortly after it began, Hasnah's worried father took her to the city of Chtaura to visit an ophthalmic expert, Dr Araji. The doctor was amazed by what he saw, and certified that the crystals were real, and that they were definitely forming in Hasnah's eyes. He could find no scientific explanation for the mystery and declared that it must be an act of God.

The phenomenon attracted huge publicity. Journalists and television crews arrived in droves to report what was happening. In order to dispel any doubts, Hasnah and her family allowed the process to be filmed in close-up, at the moment at which a crystal actually appeared from within her eye. Religious authorities competed with scientific figures to offer a plausible explanation to the public, and to capitalize on the event.

An unexpected explanation was offered by Hasnah herself, however, who described how she had witnessed a vision of the mystical figure of Maitreya. She told how a figure dressed in white and sitting upon a white horse had beckoned to her as she lay in bed at night. He told her that he was a messenger from God and that he had been responsible for the phenomenon of the crystal tears. She asked whether the tears would stop and Maitreya had replied, 'When God wills.' Hasnah's brother had apparently heard his sister speaking to someone in this way, but had been unable to see who that person was.

The arrival of a great saviour or teacher has been long awaited by many of the major world religions. Although he is known by different names, his function is thought to be the same, whatever the nature of the religion. His coming is expected to be presaged by miracles and visions, such as those that befell Hasnah, and he is thought of as a kind of Messiah.

Buddhists call this teacher Maitreya Buddha, the fifth Buddha. Hindus expect the arrival of Krishna, who will arrive on horseback as the Kaki-avatar. Christians are waiting for the return of Christ, while Jews still anticipate their Messiah. Muslims also await the arrival of their Messiah, Imam Mahdi.

In her *Theosophical Glossary*, the famous psychic Madame Blavatsky told of the coming of Maitreya. She wrote about the legendary Persian saviour, Sosiosh, who appears on horseback, predicting that: 'Sosiosh, the Mazdean Saviour, who, like Vishnu, Maitreya, Buddha and others is expected to appear on a white horse at the end of the cycle to save mankind.' Interestingly, in common with both Madame Blavatsky and Hasnah, almost every civilization to have predicted the arrival of Maitreya describes him in the same way – clothed in white, and riding a white horse. Unsurprisingly, he is often referred to as 'The White Knight'.

This mystical teacher, who appears to unite the various disparate elements of world theology, has been sighted on numerous occasions all over the globe. The sightings have been followed by a series of predictions – all delivered by a British author and lecturer, Benjamin Crème – to the effect that the teachings of Maitreya will inspire humanity to forget its differences and work together to share and support each other. Crème claims to have received these utopian visions by a process of 'spiritual telepathy'.

These assertions have generated controversy – can the proclamations of one man be relied upon as evidence of this global unifying force, or are Crème's apparent visions a more calculated attempt to draw people together?

Hasnah's personal accounts would certainly seem to support Crème's claims, and the remarkable existence of the crystals still remains to be explained.

Hasnah went on to declare that she had conversed with the figure of Maitreya on several occasions, during which she had received important advice from him. At one point, he had predicted that a misfortune would befall her family, and advised them all to leave their home temporarily.

The whole family obeyed, except for one of her brothers; the next day, the young man was involved in a car crash, from which he was fortunate to escape alive. Hasnah claims that, later that night, she was reprimanded by Maitreya, who insisted that the family should all have left home together, as he had instructed.

This case has baffled many people all over the world. Inevitably, it has also attracted numerous allegations of fraud, and certainly Hasnah's far from affluent family benefited financially from all the surrounding publicity.

It should be remembered, however, that no one has been able to explain the appearance of the crystal tears – this is a medical mystery in its own right. When taken in conjunction with the visions, it really does seem that a remarkable phenomenon took place at this time.

Perhaps we should just accept that there are some occurrences in this world that we cannot explain. Maybe time will provide an answer to the questions raised by this particular case, but in the meantime we should try to be open to the possibility that miracles can, and do, occur.

MIRACLE VEGETABLES

It appears that, on a surprising number of occasions, religious messages have been found inside a fruit or vegetable. Each time this happens, it causes a commotion within the religious community, many people taking it as some sort of divine sign, sent to strengthen their faith. Others maintain that the formations are entirely natural and have no religious meaning whatsoever. The question over which line of thinking is the correct one is very difficult to answer.

In 1997, in England alone, several messages were discovered within the seed patterns of aubergines. In February, a London grocer, Mr Sidat, was slicing an aubergine when he observed that the distribution of the seeds spelt out the word 'Allah' (God), according to Arabic script. The Sidat family interpreted this discovery as a blessing, and shared the vegetable among relatives and friends.

Just a few months later, further discoveries, again in aubergines, attracted an even greater level of public attention. On this occasion, two apparent miracles occurred simultaneously in different parts of the same Hindu community.

In two separate families, aubergines were sliced and, amazingly, the Hindu symbol for 'God' could be seen upon each of the pieces. The vegetables were deemed to be so incredible that they were displayed at local temples, where hundreds of worshippers came to witness the miraculous message.

Later in the year, a far more complex communication was discovered within a tomato. A 14-year-old schoolgirl, Shaista Javed, sliced the fruit in half and was amazed by what she saw. The seeds in one half of the tomato were so distributed as to spell out in Arabic script the words 'There is only one God', while those in the other spelt out 'Mohammed is the messenger'. These findings aroused great interest within the religious community, although the religious leaders at the local mosque were anxious not to portray it as an actual miracle.

Sceptics have argued that the discoveries should be attributed to pure coincidence, asserting that the curved lines and organic formation of both Arabic writing and Hindu symbols could appear to be echoed within the seed patterns to be found in natural objects.

It comes as no surprise that a high proportion of the so-called 'miracle' discoveries have been made by members of these two religions. By contrast, it is unlikely that any religious messages would be found by members of those religions whose language is written in a more angular script, as the sharp angles and separation of the letters bear very little correlation to anything found in nature.

This argument has, however, failed to discourage the fervent belief of those who view the discoveries as a direct message from God. The strength of feeling is such that it is unlikely that one side will ever be able to change the mind of the other. So it must be left entirely to the individual to decide which line of thinking to take: either the findings should be attributed to coincidence, or else they are examples of small miracles, revealed to the faithful. Either way, the discoveries are remarkable in their ability to perplex and astound.

MEDICAL MARVELS

Many hitherto little-understood conditions can now be treated and often cured. Nevertheless, some disorders are so bizarre and so rare that explanations are denied us. Although the human body is wonderfully complex, it cannot compare with the intricate nature of the human mind. As our understanding of disease processes improves, we hope to better understand the mysterious complexities of the human brain. It is only by recognizing these mysteries, in whatever curious form they take, that human suffering will be alleviated and mankind will make further advances.

SUPERHUMAN POWERS

There can hardly be a person alive who has not dreamed of possessing superhuman powers at some point in their lives. What is truly amazing is the fact that these abilities have actually been shown to exist outside the world of fiction, and are in evidence even today.

Throughout history, certain groups of warriors have earned themselves fearsome reputations for their incredible strength and martial invulnerability. There is no doubt that these warriors revelled in this image of themselves, and benefited from a psychological advantage on the battlefield. In many cases, however, their reputation would be based on genuinely extraordinary powers.

The Berserkers were among the most terrifying groups of warriors ever to wage war on Europe – it is from their very ferocity that the word 'berserk' is derived. Originating from Scandinavia, the Berserkers essentially became the elite fighting force of the Vikings, renowned for their immunity to weapons. To demonstrate this invulnerability, they were said to head into battle without armour or even chain mail, and to fight like raging beasts.

There is little doubt that, to a large extent, the status enjoyed by the Berserkers could be attributed simply to their unparalleled ferocity in battle. A warrior who ignored his wounds, no matter how grave, and continued to fight would have been a terrifying adversary. It is entirely possible, however, that these warriors did not actually feel their wounds, having been worked up into such a state of bloodlust that they were able to overlook their injuries until the battle was over and they had calmed down from their furious state.

Alternatively, the Berserkers' invulnerability in battle could have been achieved by performing spells or rituals prior to engaging the enemy. This might have induced in them an altered, trance-like state in which they could avoid sensations of pain, or at least postpone them until they were ready. Whatever the means by which they achieved their remarkable powers, it was highly effective, as the accounts of their vanquished foes attest.

The Berserkers were not the only group of warriors to be known for their immunity to pain, and invulnerability to weapons. The Rufa Dervishes were feared and respected by friend and foe alike, and it is testament to their reputation that they are immortalised in a phrase ('whirling dervish') that describes their ferocity and aggression.

These words also hint at the root of their powers, which, according to reliable reports, were induced at religious rituals in which the warriors would work themselves into a state of religious delirium or ecstatic trance, known as Halah. In a frantic celebration of their ability to deny pain, the Dervishes would carry out the widespread self-infliction of wounds throughout the group. They might grasp hold of white-hot irons or place hot coals in their mouths that would glow as the men breathed and were even said to pierce themselves with special spikes. Following this ecstatic frenzy, a healing ritual would take place, with the Shiakh of the group breathing upon each man's wounds and praying. Within a day, even the most life-threatening of the injuries would have healed.

The Dervishes entered battle as supremely confident warriors, with a strong belief in their own invulnerability. This would be particularly advantageous when the fighting was at its height, since the warriors held any injury in contempt and so earned a reputation for outstanding bravery.

The battlefield is not the only arena where such superhuman powers have been displayed, however – sometimes, they can be applied in a much more peaceful way. Spiritual figures such as Tibetan monks and Indian Yogis are able to control their bodies in ways that seem utterly beyond comprehension. Onlookers have been captivated by their remarkable ability to stay alive in the most inhospitable environments, or by their displays of amazing physical prowess.

Some of the monks of the Tibetan Himalayas seem able to defy the extreme cold of their environment. In a system known as 'tummo' (inner fire), they undertake extensive training in the form of numerous hours of meditation every day, focusing intently on the flame of warmth within their own bodies. When they are deemed to have mastered this ability, the monks face a dangerous test that, if they are not sufficiently prepared, may prove fatal.

Although this test involves nothing more than sitting in silent meditation, it is its location that is the real challenge. The monks meditate outside in the bitter cold of the mountains, wearing only a thin tunic that has been soaked in freezing water. The test requires the monk to render the tunic completely dry using just the heat from his body.

Only when the monk has performed this seemingly impossible feat three times in one sitting is he considered to have passed the test. He will then wear nothing more than just the thin tunic, having demonstrated that he has no need for any warmer clothing. The fact that human beings can accomplish such tasks is truly incredible and yet the practice is about much more than the simple generation of warmth.

The entire system is an ideology in itself. The monks believe that, in releasing the heat from their bodies, they are burning away spiritual impurities such as envy or ignorance and refreshing their spirit. They maintain that a healthy mind will lead to a healthy body, and in many respects they have been proved right. Notwithstanding the deeper meaning behind this exercise, the fact remains that these holy men have completely shifted the boundaries of what is considered possible for a human being.

Much of the most unusual evidence of supernormal powers comes from the Yogis of India. In the 1950s, researchers at the Menninger Foundation in Kansas, USA, came across one Yogi who could produce a voluntary heart fibrillation that was measured at 306 beats per minute. Such speeds are rarely recorded in humans at their peak of adrenalized exertion. The same Yogi had such incredible control over the microscopic functions of his own body that he could also dramatically alter its temperature. In a stunning display, he was able to make one side of his palm overheat, while the other would grow grey with cold. In effect, he had induced a temperature differential in this hand of 12°C.

Another, perhaps, even more famous example of the abilities of the Yogis was publicized in a 1974 photograph, which depicted a Yogi who

A Yogi in Rajasthan, practising physical control.

was apparently still alive even though his head was buried beneath sand. According to witnesses, he had stopped breathing completely and had reduced his heartbeat to just two beats a minute. In this condition, he could survive with his head buried for days at a time.

This minute and precise control of reflex actions was not believed possible until the mid-20th century, when science at last provided an explanation. The Yogis are able to achieve these feats through the power of meditation alone, which enables them to lower their metabolism, control their body temperature, heartbeat and even the electrical activity in their brains. It has been reported that certain Yogis are also capable of levitation.

Such dramatic displays of control demonstrate the mysterious power of the human brain, which is accessible to some of those who have dedicated their lives to the achievement of an advanced meditative state. This superhuman ability offers a tantalising glimpse to the rest of humanity of the amazing potential that lurks within the furthest reaches of human consciousness which, for now, lies out of the reach of the majority of humankind.

'ALICE IN WONDERLAND SYNDROME'

The peculiar condition known as 'Alice in Wonderland Syndrome' drastically affects the visual and mental perception of the sufferer. Characteristic of the syndrome is a completely distorted sense of time, distance, size and space, that can leave the patient totally disorientated and in a state of serious distress. Little is understood about the cause of the condition, although doctors believe that it can be linked in some way to better known afflictions.

The syndrome was first diagnosed in 1955 by an English psychiatrist, John Todd. Finding the symptoms of the illness amazingly far-fetched, he named it after Lewis Carroll's famous book, although the condition has also occasionally been termed 'Lilliputian hallucination', after the tiny characters of Robert Swift's book *Gulliver's Travels*. The fact that both terms are borrowed from fantasy fiction is testament to the bizarre nature of the illness.

A patient with 'Alice in Wonderland Syndrome' will typically also be a sufferer of migraine headaches, which are believed to be linked in some way to the condition. Strangely, it is recorded that Lewis Carroll himself actually suffered from severe migraines for most of his life. Could it be possible that Carroll suffered from this condition himself, and that his own symptoms provided him with the inspiration for his classic novel?

It seems likely, as a number of the condition's symptoms are mirrored in the story of what happens to Alice. Just as, after eating and drinking two separate magical concoctions, Alice becomes first tiny, and then larger than a house, so those with this syndrome may experience similar distortions – a form of visual and sensory hallucination can make them feel as if their entire body, or sometimes just parts of it, have grown or shrunk in scale. Problems that result from this, such as feelings of invulnerability or paranoia, can place a patient in serious danger.

To date, no thorough explanation of this condition has been offered, although the theory regarding its link with migraine headaches is believed to be sound.

In common with other strange medical phenomena, one of the obstacles to research is the scarcity of cases. So few people with this syndrome have existed that it is very difficult to compare and contrast different cases. Without doubt, this is one of the most unusual conditions ever to test the powers of medical science. Will scientists, in the years ahead, be able to solve it?

THE FALLON CANCER CLUSTER

Fallon, a small agricultural town in Nevada, is similar in many ways to hundreds of other towns across the USA. One fact, however, sets it apart. Despite its population of just 7,500, Fallon has one of the largest proportions of cancer sufferers in the USA. Moreover, almost all of those affected have been children, diagnosed with leukaemia.

It took some time before doctors realized that such a pattern was forming within the community, and they were mystified as to how this could have occurred, as leukaemia is not a contagious disease. They started a desperate search for a common denominator between the cases – if this factor were to be found, then it could be investigated in depth, but without it, the task would be enormous.

Accordingly, each affected family was interviewed at length, and asked detailed questions about anything that might have had an impact on their health. Doctors even noted all the cleaning products and chemicals that were kept in their homes. However, the search proved inconclusive – it seemed that the only link between the cancer patients was the fact that they lived, or had once lived, in Fallon.

This immediately led doctors to believe that there must be something about the town that was causing such an incidence of illness among its inhabitants. Their investigation of the area revealed several possible causes, although none of these has ever been proved conclusively, and of course there is always the chance that a combination of factors could be to blame.

One of the favoured theories about the Fallon cancer cluster is that the town might have been subjected to some form of contamination from the huge naval air base that is located only 16km (10 miles) away. Large numbers of military personnel pass through the air base in order to undertake fighter jet training over the Nevada Desert. Thus, contamination could occur in one of two ways: firstly, the huge flow of people through the air base could introduce a wide variety of viruses or illnesses into the small community; and secondly, the vast quantities of aviation fuel used by the base could pollute the environment to such an extent that serious illness could have resulted.

Although research on cats and cows has shown that viral infections can cause leukaemia in animals, no test has ever shown that this is possible in humans. It might be, however, that there has to be an element of genetic susceptibility present before such a situation can arise. European research studies have proved that the health of residents of small towns can be adversely affected by large influxes of people, as their immune systems have not become acclimatized to the wide variety of illnesses introduced to the community. It is possible, therefore, that an unusual virus found its way into Fallon via the air base, and then went on to have a disastrous effect on the vulnerable population.

The second, more likely, possibility is based upon the notion that some type of environmental pollution could have taken place. The air base, home to the US Navy's 'Top Gun' school that was made famous in the film of the same name, uses a reported 155 million litres of fuel every year. The exhaust emissions from this quantity of fuel are undoubtedly significant. In addition to this, all of the aviation fuel used flows through a pipeline travelling directly under the town of Fallon. Although no leak in this pipeline has ever been suspected or found, the likelihood cannot be ruled out completely.

When further investigations into military activity in the area were carried out, however, the theory of fuel contamination actually paled into insignificance next to something altogether more sinister.

Back in 1963, the American military conducted 'Project Shoal', the trial detonation of a 13-kiloton nuclear bomb, in an underground test site in the Sand Mountain range, less than 50km (31 miles) from Fallon. It is well known that previous nuclear explosions, such as those at Hiroshima and Chernobyl, have led to an increased incidence of cancer locally.

Official reports, however, state that no radiation from this experiment should ever have endangered Fallon for, among other factors, the depth at which the test was carried out would have prevented any possible contamination from radioactive fall-out.

Nevertheless, the fact still remains that a nuclear test was performed very close to the town and, although more than 40 years have passed, it will be many thousands of years before the radioactive contamination completely fades from the site.

It has also been established that, of all the towns in the USA, Fallon has some of the highest levels of naturally occurring arsenic in its water supply. Having said that, the authorities maintain that the arsenic is still not present in sufficient quantities to endanger health, and it should also be remembered that prior to the discovery of the cancer cluster the water had been drunk by several generations of residents without any recorded ill effects. Nevertheless, it has been suggested that the problem might only have become evident after sufficient time had passed to allow the traces of arsenic to build up to a level that might cause harm.

Further tests upon the natural environment around Fallon have revealed the presence of mercury – a highly toxic heavy metal – in a nearby lake and irrigation canals.

Similarly threatening are some of the fertilizers and pesticides that would have been used in large quantities in the mainly agricultural community of Fallon.

Over a period of several generations, trace elements of these toxins could have built up to such an extent in the food chain that they posed a threat to human health.

To date, there has been no official explanation for the cancer cluster at Fallon. With so many harmful substances present in the area, however, the possibility that the cases have arisen due to contamination of the local environment seems quite likely. Moreover, it is even possible that further, secret, contamination might have taken place here.

In addition to 'Project Shoal', the US military could have carried out other tests in this remote area of Nevada that, due to the inherent need for military secrecy, especially throughout the Cold War, were never revealed to the public.

Alternatively, as some scientists have suggested, such cancer clusters may just exist naturally and perhaps there is nothing unusual about the situation in Fallon, other than the level of misfortune for those concerned.

With no definitive explanation offered by science, the case remains a mystery. Perhaps time will provide an answer – in the meantime, it can only be hoped that the tragic fate that befell the town of Fallon will not be repeated elsewhere.

'JUMPING FRENCHMAN OF MAINE' SYNDROME

'Jumping Frenchman of Maine' syndrome is a peculiar condition in which the patient displays an exaggerated reflex reaction as a result of the alarm or panic arising from even the smallest of shocks. A typical response involves leaping, shrieking and waving the arms and, in some cases, the patient adopts the foetal position. All of these reactions are generally grossly disproportionate to the actual shock involved.

The condition was first diagnosed in 1878 by an American physician, Dr Beard, who recorded his discoveries in a dispatch to the American Neurological Association. He based his diagnosis on studies of a small number of French-Canadian lumberjacks from the Moosehead Lake area of Maine, USA – it is from here that part of the name originates.

Dr Beard also noted another strange response in many of these patients – the involuntary reflexive obedience to sudden or sharp commands. For instance, the order to strike someone would be immediately obeyed without a conscious thought for the consequences of this action, even if it were carried out against a friend or family member. Patients who suffered from this particular trait would often echo the words that had been uttered. Some would even do this when they were spoken to in another language, repeating the phrase immediately without understanding its meaning.

It was found that, for the vast majority of sufferers, the onset of symptoms began soon after they had started working as a lumberjack, suggesting that the logging work might have induced the condition in some way.

Investigations into this apparent link attempted to discover some kind of neurotoxin in the flora and fungi of the forest, or perhaps an insect, that might be the cause of the unusual behaviour. However, to date, nothing has been discovered to prove a connection, although it remains a potential explanation.

Doctors now believe that the syndrome is not actually neurological in its origins, but is, in fact, a psychological condition. In the early days of research, it was thought to be allied to Tourette's syndrome, but although there are certain similarities between the two disorders, 'Jumping Frenchman of Maine' syndrome is a distinctive condition in its own right.

Extreme stress has been suggested as a cause of the condition, after comparisons were made between its symptoms and those of First World War soldiers suffering from 'shell shock', in whom loud noises prompted a similar response. This was rejected, however, because there was apparently nothing in the loggers' environment that could bring about such levels of stress.

It is more likely that the syndrome is genetic in origin, as the majority of sufferers seem to have come from small, isolated communities in which there may have been some inbreeding within families, such as the loggers of Maine and, most recently, among men living in the Beauce region of Quebec.

Until more cases of this rare condition are uncovered and studied, it is unlikely that the true explanation for such an unusual affliction will be revealed.

For now, the cause of the disorder remains as much of a mystery as the identity of the original 'jumping Frenchman of Maine'.

TREPANNING

The practice of trepanning – the cutting or drilling of a hole through a patient's skull – can be traced back to the days of our ancient ancestors and is still performed in a limited way today. Although its purpose is primarily medical, trepanning could be said to straddle both the scientific and mystical spectrums as it also has a spiritual application.

Some of the earliest examples of trepanning can be traced back as far as 4,000 years ago, when it was performed by early Peruvian Indians from the Inca and pre-Inca societies. When the first skulls containing holes were discovered, it was initially thought that these were as a result of fatal head wounds acquired in conflict. On closer inspection, however, archaeologists realized that some of the skull holes had been cut with great precision and many of them showed signs of bone regeneration, meaning that the person involved had survived the procedure.

Archaeologists realized that a type of surgery must have been performed on these people, although quite how primitive man managed to achieve this with tools made from rock and flint, and no form of antiseptic, is nothing short of remarkable.

The fact that skulls bearing the tell-tale holes of trepanning have been discovered on almost every continent of the world indicates not only how widespread this incredibly dangerous practice was, but also that man must have become very skilled at it, with so many patients obviously surviving surgery.

By the early 1900s, when trepanning was practised quite frequently, the technique had advanced so much that precise tools were being crafted specifically for the task. Scalpels and circular drill-saws were regularly used to reduce the likelihood of splintering bone or damaging the brain during the operation.

Throughout the ages trepanning has been performed for a number of reasons, some of which are still behind the practice today. Firstly, there were purely medical forms of trepanation, which would have been carried out to relieve pressure on the brain and so save the person's life. A warrior with head wounds, for example, might have been treated in this way. This type of surgery, still practised as an emergency procedure today, indicates the remarkable level of understanding of anatomy and medicine possessed by primitive man.

Secondly, some trepanations were performed in an attempt to cure head-related maladies such as migraine, epilepsy or mental illness. The practice was not carried out with a genuine understanding of the ailment itself, but rather in an attempt to expel demons or evil spirits that were thought to dwell inside the head of the sufferer. This has a resonance with what is known of primitive man's ideas of possession by demons, and it is believed that the operation actually continued for these reasons as late as the Middle Ages in Europe. It may even still be carried out by remote civilizations in some parts of the world.

Thirdly, there is somewhat grim evidence to show that trepanning was performed for purposes such as the creation of jewellery or magical implements and could have been inflicted on unwilling subjects such as prisoners. Talismans have been recovered from Bolivia and Peru consisting of several discs of human skull, polished and perforated and then strung on a necklace, which was supposedly imbued with the power to protect the wearer.

Finally, trepanning has also been carried out for quasi-religious reasons, as part of an exercise in expanding consciousness in order perhaps to acquire mystical powers. It is known that our ancestors, with their interest in shamanism and sacrifice, had a particularly strong sense of the supernatural and it is likely that trepanning would have been performed as part of a ritual for the purposes of entering an altered state of mind.

There has been a limited resurgence of interest in this last application today, with some people successfully performing self-trepanation in order to achieve a state of enlightenment similar to that sought by primitive man. There are several documented cases of such practices, some even cutting holes into their heads with electric drills. Although the procedure is criticized by the medical profession – as it puts the person at risk of blood poisoning, cerebral meningitis, lobotomy or even death – enthusiasts speak highly of it, claiming that it has, in fact, enhanced their level of consciousness.

A prime devotee of self-trepanation is a Dutchman named Bart Hughes, the founder of the New World Trepanation Movement. He managed to successfully conduct a self-trepanation as far back as the 1960s, after forming his own theory about the functions of the brain. Like many spiritually inclined people before and after him, Hughes was seeking to discover a higher level of awareness, which he associated with the mindset of childhood. He believed that children have greater powers of imagination and perception, and this stems from the nature of their skulls.

When a child is born, its skull is formed of several plates that expand through childhood to allow growth. Only once a person reaches adulthood does the skull actually harden and solidify. Hughes maintained that this ossification of the skull inhibits cerebral processes by restricting the flow of blood and oxygen to the brain. He believed that through self-trepanation he had liberated his brain and his consciousness from his restrictive skull and claimed to feel immediate benefits, saying that he felt as a child once more, his brain having the room to pulse with his heartbeat.

Hughes was so enamoured with his discovery that he expounded its benefits to the world at a press conference. This concerned the authorities, and they subsequently placed Hughes in a mental asylum for observation. This did not, however, prevent a number of people from following his teachings and from repeating the experiment at home on themselves.

Although the medical establishment dismisses the alleged spiritual benefits of trepanation as being due to nothing more than the power of faith healing, perhaps it really can enhance an individual's consciousness, concentration and intelligence, as has been claimed.

EXTREME PHYSICAL ABNORMALITIES

Throughout history, there have been individuals who have stood out from the rest of mankind as a result of their extreme physical abnormalities. Although in previous times, society has often ridiculed and mistreated those who look so out of the ordinary, today such treatment is frowned upon and discouraged.

The world's endless appetite for the strange and unusual has, however, brought many such individuals into the spotlight, and even turned some of them into celebrities in their own right – the case of the so-called 'elephant man' is one example. History has produced some extraordinary characters, whose very existence is a total mystery.

One such individual, Pasqual Pinon, achieved a degree of fame in the early years of the 20th century. For three years he was effectively a star performer in the Sells-Floto Circus sideshow due entirely to the fact that he possessed two heads, a condition known as craniopagus parasite. Rather than having two necks, the second of his heads protruded from the top of his skull, and was about half the size of his main head.

According to the advertisements used to promote his travelling show, Pinon was a Mexican labourer who had fled his country – following General Pershing to Texas – after raids by the Mexican rebel Pancho Villa had destroyed his livelihood. Pinon claimed that his second head could behave independently of the other head and had functioning senses of sight and smell. He also alleged that, up until the age of 20, he was able to speak through the mouth of the second head. At this age, however, he suffered a debilitating stroke, which left the head immobile and in a state of atrophy.

Medical science has been suspicious of this claim, as it would appear to differ markedly from anything seen before or since. Although there have been other recorded cases of people being born with two heads, they have never been known to exist before in this kind of physical formation. On the very rare occasions when this has happened in the past, the second head has always sat upside down on top of the main head, so that the tops of the two skulls are joined together. An example of this 'mirror image' effect can be seen in the miraculous 'Two-Headed Boy of Bengal', and more recently in a girl born in the Dominican Republic, Rebeca Martinez.

Scientists have therefore concluded that Pinon was either a remarkable new case, the likelihood of which should not be discounted given the rare nature of these conditions, or that he was in some way faking his abnormality. If the latter were true, though, he would have had to put in a great deal of effort to produce what was certainly a very convincing appearance of having two heads. One possibility is that the protrusion from the top of his skull may have been not a second head at all, but an unusual type of tumour. He might then have attached a waxen face to the front of this large lump, and invented the curious story of his youth.

If Pinon was guilty of enhancing his deformity to increase his earning potential, then he would not have been the first person to act in this way. Another star of the sideshow was William Durks, who claimed to have not two heads, but two faces. In reality, however, Durks had a cleft mouth and a split nose. Although only one of his eyes functioned properly, he would add a false third eye to the middle of his face, thus creating the effect of having two faces.

Certain individuals have required no such adjustment of their physical appearance to mystify their audiences. Siamese (conjoined) twins are a rare natural abnormality, occurring as a result of an incomplete separation in the womb of a single fertilized egg. The term originates from the first widely publicized case of such twins, Chang and Eng, who were born in Siam and went on to become celebrities in their own right, performing throughout the 19th century. The twins lived for more than 60 years, and both eventually married, fathering 21 children between them.

The most famous European from this period of history with such a condition was Jean Libbera. Born in Rome in 1884, Libbera performed under the title of 'The Man with Two Bodies'. In certain cases of conjoined twins, the incomplete division of the egg in the womb results in only one normal sized person, the other twin failing to develop fully into an individual.

This was the essence of Libbera's condition, for he had an almost fully formed body attached to his own, from the shoulders down. His vestigial twin was attached to Libbera's torso by the neck and shoulders, with a small semi-formed skull actually located within Libbera's body itself.

Medical science termed the second twin an 'epigastric parasite' as, although it was formed of living tissue, it survived by feeding from Libbera's system.

There is still a great deal to be understood about the functions and workings of the human body, which is a machine so complex as to be incomprehensible at times. For centuries, mankind has been fascinated by mysteries that lie within our own bodies and, of all the world's great unknowns, perhaps it is this that is the most remarkable.

'WALKING CORPSE' SYNDROME

Cotard's syndrome is a particularly dangerous and unpleasant disorder. Also known as 'Walking Corpse' syndrome, it is usually associated with a serious depressive state, and frequently involves psychosis. The main symptom of the condition is the patient's absolute conviction that he or she is dead.

The condition takes its name from the French doctor, Jules Cotard, who first diagnosed the condition in 1880, calling it *'delire des negations'* (delusion of negation). It is possible, however, that the syndrome was discovered almost a century prior to this. In 1788 a man named Charles Bonnet spoke of a case in which a woman was so convinced of her own death that she lay in a coffin, dressed in a shroud. She even requested that she be buried, but no one would consent to this. She refused to move from the coffin, remaining there for several weeks until she actually was dead.

It seems likely that this woman did suffer from Cotard's syndrome because of the nature of her delusions, although these can be many and varied. Patients might believe that only part of their body is dead or perhaps that just their spirit has departed. They might feel as if their body is no more than a shell, or that they have turned to stone. Or, even more bizarrely, the hallucinatory convictions might be so powerful that sufferers actually describe the smell of their own rotting flesh, or the sensation of worms crawling through their skin. Treatment of patients with this bizarre condition is a complex and challenging process.

Although, in many cases, sufferers otherwise function normally and rationally, the delusions over their mortality can place them, and those around them, in serious danger. Some individuals have committed suicide, or tried to do so, in an attempt to prove that they are genuinely dead. Others remain totally convinced of their own invulnerability, believing that, as they are dead, they can come to no harm.

Most patients with this disorder will, in physical terms at least, be perfectly healthy. However, in a prime example of the power of the human mind, the nature of the condition can often have a serious effect on bodily health – patients have been known to starve themselves, believing food unnecessary for them, or even attempt to amputate their own limbs.

Although the preoccupation with mortality that is a hallmark of this condition can be found in other areas of severe mental illness, the fact remains that Cotard's syndrome is rare. Treatment today still focuses more on containment than on cure, but it is hoped that the growing pace of medical discovery will one day offer real hope to those affected by this curious disorder.

CURSES

Curses are essentially a form of magic spell uttered with the intention of harming a person or place. Over time, vast numbers of curses have been passed, fuelling superstition around these unseen and inexplicable forces. Many students of science who pour scorn on the idea of a curse will nevertheless have a lucky mascot on their desks when they sit their examinations. This is really no more than a modern equivalent of the talisman, believed by our ancestors to bestow magical powers on the wearer and to protect against misfortune. Whether or not curses do have an effect on the cursed, it is true to say that their power will remain as long as people continue to believe in them.

'THE LITTLE BASTARD'

James Dean, the iconic Hollywood film star, died tragically young, at a point in his life when his acting career was going from strength to strength. Although he had starred in only a few films, he had earned himself much acclaim and a sizeable fortune.

With his new-found riches, Dean had bought a sports car, a Porsche Spyder, one of only 90 in the world at that time. He nicknamed the car 'The Little Bastard', and had this name painted on the machine along with a racing stripe.

Dean had intended to race his beloved car himself, but sadly never had the chance. On 30 September 1955, only two weeks after he had bought the car, he died in it, following a head-on collision with another vehicle. The driver of the other car survived, having sustained only cuts and bruises.

In the weeks preceding his death, Dean had been seen driving his car everywhere, proudly displaying it to all of his friends, although he was surprised to find that many of them failed to share his enthusiasm for the powerful machine.

Several of them apparently felt a sense of horror when they saw the vehicle – some out of concern for the dangers that such a fast car might pose to Dean's reckless nature, others simply because of an innate sense of foreboding about the machine.

At the time, Dean would not have been aware that a number of strange happenings had already been linked with the car since its arrival at the Competition Motors showroom. Several mechanics had hurt themselves on the car shortly after it was delivered, one breaking his thumb after trapping it in one of the doors and another cutting himself as he adjusted the engine. At the time, these events seemed to be no more than accidents, but later they would be seen as part of a much larger pattern of misfortune, or even something altogether more sinister.

After the fatal crash, the car wreckage was bought for salvage by the motor mechanic George Barris, the very man who had customized the machine for Dean several weeks earlier. It was only when he began to re-use parts of the car that he started to suspect that some form of terrible curse might be attached to the vehicle, a curse that had not only claimed the life of the young film star, but was also causing numerous other disasters in the lives of those unlucky enough to have acquired a piece of the car.

The engine of 'The Little Bastard' had been largely undamaged by the crash, so Barris had reconditioned it and sold it to a racing enthusiast, Dr William F. Eschrich.

One of the doctor's friends and fellow racer, Dr Carl McHenry, learned of the sale and decided to buy the transaxle of the car. Barris also sold several other vehicle parts, including the two back tyres.

In the first race in which the two doctors tested their new equipment, both men were involved in serious accidents. Dr Eschrich's car turned over after locking up on entering a bend. Fortunately he survived the crash, although he was left paralyzed. Dr McHenry was not so lucky: he was killed after losing control of the car and hitting a tree. As if this were not enough, before the week was out, the driver who had bought the two back tyres narrowly escaped death after both tyres blew out simultaneously during another race.

Learning of the multiple disasters, Barris decided that he would try to put the car to some kind of beneficial use. Accordingly, he lent the crumpled machine to the California Highway Safety Patrol for publicity purposes, thinking that Dean's fame would greatly enhance their campaign on accident prevention. Unfortunately, at that point he did not realize that the car was actually a source of accidents in itself.

The car was taken into the possession of the Highway Patrol and stored in a garage with a large number of other cars. While it was there, a mysterious fire broke out – many cars were completely destroyed and almost all incurred serious damage. Curiously, 'The Little Bastard' emerged from the fire remarkably unscathed.

A short time later, while the car was being taken to a display area for demonstration purposes, a strange accident took place. Dean's car was being transported on the back of a flat-bed truck, driven by an experienced driver named George Barhuis, when it skidded on a wet road, and the truck's rig crashed into a ditch. Barhuis was thrown from the cab by the impact, but is believed to have survived the crash. However, in a bewildering tragedy, he was then killed when the wreck of 'The Little Bastard' fell from the back of the truck and landed on top of him, crushing him to death.

Yet the litany of disasters was still not complete. On the fourth anniversary of Dean's fatal crash, a teenager in Detroit was viewing the car, which was on a large display. Without warning, the structure on which the car was resting collapsed, and the car toppled forwards crushing the boy's legs. It seems inconceivable that, following this, the car was still put out on display to the public.

A few weeks after this accident, the car was once again being transported by truck, when it fell from the back of the vehicle, smashing into the road and causing the serious injury of yet more people.

Fortunately, the cursed car was doomed itself. Shortly after this final accident, the vehicle spontaneously fell apart while on show in New Orleans. Attempts were made to put it back together, but George Barris stepped in and arranged to have the remains of the car transported back to his garage in California. When the delivery arrived, the container was opened and, to their astonishment, the car had disappeared.

It is not known if it had been stolen by an obsessive admirer of the film star, but no trace of it has ever been found. Certainly, if anyone had been foolish enough to take the vehicle into their own possession, they would have been very fortunate to escape the curse that had randomly struck at those connected with the car. Nevertheless, the fact that it is now missing can only add to the sense of mystery that surrounds not only this jinxed machine, but also the tragic, doomed figure of James Dean.

THE BLACK HOPE CURSE

Some curses are so general that they are feared by large numbers of people or entire populations. Trinkets and lucky charms are often worn as a means of self-protection. Other curses are more specific, directed at a particular person, group or place – often these individual stories become woven into the very fabric of superstition, reinforcing the notion that such malevolent powers do, in fact, exist.

This type of personal experience was certainly the case as far as the Haney and Williams families were concerned, when they bought their brand-new homes near Houston, Texas, in 1982. Moving into the neighbourhood was the culmination of their family dreams, as their houses were set in large gardens on an attractive new estate.

One year after the move, Sam and Judith Haney appeared to have settled well into their new home. This was all to change, however, when they decided to have a swimming pool built in their garden. Digging commenced, whereupon an elderly man living in the area knocked on their door and brought them some unsettling news.

He informed them that their new house was built on the site of an old African-American burial ground and that, in excavating part of the garden for the swimming pool, they were digging precisely over some of the graves. He even gave the Haneys the names of some black families who used to live in the area so that they could corroborate his story. The Haneys, however, were sceptical and continued work on the pool.

After a short while, two crude coffins were unearthed, containing the remains of a man and a woman. Appalled by their discovery, the Haneys realized that the old man had been right. Once the shock had settled, they decided that it was imperative that the bodies should be returned to their resting place with a proper burial.

So they set about trying to establish the identity of the bodies. Their search culminated in the discovery of an elderly man, Jasper Norton, who had worked as a gravedigger within the former black community. He informed the Haneys that the housing estate on which they lived was indeed built on the site of a former cemetery which had been named Black Hope, and contained mainly the graves of slaves. He identified the exhumed bodies as belonging to two slaves, Charlie and Betty Thomas, who had died when he was a young man.

The Haneys continued their search, this time for descendants of the buried couple. When this proved fruitless, they decided to return the remains to the spot from which they had come. They were troubled at having disturbed a grave, and hoped that, by reburial, they could lay the whole episode to rest – as events were to reveal, however, they were very much mistaken.

Not long after they had reburied the bodies, the Haneys' lives began to be affected by strange happenings. At first, this took the form of disembodied voices that disturbed their nightly sleep, but soon there were other incidents such as appliances and lights spontaneously turning on and off, further unnatural noises and the discovery of a pair of Judith Haney's shoes on the very spot where Betty Thomas lay buried.

After a while, the Haneys' fear and bewilderment grew to such an extent that they confided in their neighbours, Ben and Jean Williams. To their amazement, they discovered that they were not the only family to have suffered from paranormal interventions – at least a dozen of the households had experienced some kind of unexplained activity, ranging from doors opening and closing to strange apparitions.

Like the Haneys, the Williams family also believed that they were being persecuted by a curse from beyond the grave. Although they had not themselves actually found any corpses on their land, they had been astonished to find that nothing seemed to grow in their garden, and that strange, deep holes would continually appear, forming afresh even after they had been filled in. This belief turned to outright conviction when six members of the Williams family were diagnosed with cancer in the same year – sadly, for three of them, this was fatal. As far as the Williams family were concerned, this was a direct intervention from beyond the grave.

Events took an even more tragic turn when Jean Williams decided to find out whether there were any graves in her garden, such as there were on the Haneys' land. So one day she and her daughter, Tina, started to dig up the garden. After a short while, Tina collapsed. Two days later, she died from a heart attack, aged just 30.

Could it be that these two families were right and that the dead had objected so strongly to the desecration of their graves that they had managed to bridge the gap between their world and ours? For the residents of the former Black Hope cemetery, there was no question. They believed that the land was cursed, and that they had activated this curse by disturbing the graves.

Events proved too much for the Haney and Williams families, who decided to sell up and move on. Whatever force had been acting upon them, whether it was the workings of their own subconscious or the 'Black Hope Curse' itself, several lives had been lost and many families had been driven from their homes in fear.

Curiously, subsequent tenants of their former homes did not report any problems at all. Had the spirits' anger been satisfied, or had the unpleasant knowledge that they lived above a graveyard just been too much for the 'cursed' families? If events had been restricted solely to the occasional strange happening within the households, then perhaps they could have been accused of paranoia. The extent of the illnesses and deaths involved, however, seem to make the case for a curse a rather convincing one.

CHIEF CORNSTALK

For many years the area of West Virginia known as Point Pleasant has been beset by a series of disasters and misfortunes. Although these could be attributed to nothing more than bad luck, some ascribe the events to the ancient curse of a betrayed Native American chief.

In order to understand the nature and power of a curse, it is necessary to know the background to the events – only then can it be judged whether there could have been sufficient cause for such a potent force of revenge.

The story in this particular case dates back more than 200 years, to the 1770s, when the American frontiersmen were battling against the Native Americans in their attempts to push west, and later fighting the British for their independence.

As the American settlers found their way to the land around the Ohio River, now West Virginia, they encountered strong resistance from Native American tribes, some of whom had joined together to form a powerful confederacy. This was led by the chieftain of the Shawnee tribe, a man called Keigh-tugh-gua (Cornstalk).

A battle between the American settlers and the Native Americans took place in 1774, and both sides sustained heavy losses. The Native Americans were forced to retreat westwards as the settlers took over the land and fortified it. Cornstalk, recognizing that he would have trouble defeating such heavily armed men, decided to make peace with them.

A few years later, trouble was to erupt again, as the British began to stir up feeling against the rebellious settlers. They tried to bring as many Native Americans on to their side as possible and several tribes from Cornstalk's old confederacy joined them to prepare an attack on the settlements. Cornstalk chose instead to honour his peace and he and Chief Red Hawk of the Delaware tribe, went to the American fort to discuss the situation.

On their arrival, the chieftains were taken hostage by the Americans, as it was believed that the tribes would not attack while their chiefs were being held. While in captivity, Cornstalk was well treated, and even assisted the American settlers in planning their tactics against the British. After a few days, Cornstalk's young son, Ellinipisco, came to the fort with news for his father, whereupon he was also taken hostage.

Shortly after this, events took a dramatic turn for the worse after a number of American soldiers who had gone out to hunt deer were ambushed and killed by Native Americans. When this was discovered, discipline inside the fort broke down and an angry mob broke into the prisoners' quarters with murder in mind. They showed no mercy to Cornstalk or his young son, who was shot before his very eyes. It was this act of murder and betrayal that prompted Cornstalk to utter his mighty curse, words that, it seems, have affected the area for hundreds of years.

According to legend, he declared, 'I came to this fort as your friend and you murdered me. You have murdered by my side my young son. For this may the curse of the Great Spirit rest upon this land. May it be blighted by nature. May it be blighted in its hopes.'

After these tragic events had taken place, Cornstalk was afforded a proper burial, and he was interred near the fort where he had been killed. He was not allowed to rest in peace, however, since his remains were dug up and moved twice for the sake of new buildings and monuments – first in 1840, and then again in 1950. If the original act of betrayal had not been sufficient to secure the power of the curse, then the desecration of his grave surely was.

This area became known as Point Pleasant and, almost in defiance of the curse, residents decided to erect a monument in honour of the soldiers who had defeated Cornstalk in the first battle of 1774. Strangely, this monument was to be struck twice by lightning, first in 1909, delaying its unveiling ceremony, and then again in 1921, causing serious damage.

These happenings were nothing, however, compared to the catalogue of disasters that was to befall this relatively small community. In 1880 a huge fire ravaged an entire block in the centre of town, while in 1907 America's worst mining disaster was responsible for the deaths of 310 men. In 1967, the Silver Bridge disaster killed 46 people. This coincided with strange local sightings such as lights in the sky and the regular appearance of the mysterious stalker known as 'Mothman'.

Shortly after this, in 1968 and 1970, a number of aircraft crashed in the area, killing more than 100 passengers. In 1978 a derailed freight train caused an immense spill of toxic chemicals that poisoned that land and the water basin of the area, destroying all the local wells.

It is thought that this environmental catastrophe could be the blight of nature mentioned in Cornstalk's curse, while the blighting of hope appears to have been manifest in the depressed economy of Point Pleasant.

There are many who would maintain that when disaster befalls a person or community, it is just a matter of misfortune. To suggest that it is as a result of a curse, they say, is to resort to ancient superstitions which have no place in the modern world. When, however, such a huge chain of catastrophes occurs, as has been the case with Point Pleasant, it is difficult not to admit that a curse might have been responsible after all.

THE EARLS OF MAR

The ruins of Alloa Tower in Scotland are now all that remains of a vast manor, the hereditary seat of the Erskine family, the Earls of Mar. The fate of the place was interwoven with that of the family who lived there, not just because they had lived there for generations, but because of the curse that predicted and assured the doom of the family and the seat of their power.

It is believed that this curse was uttered against the Earl of Mar by the Abbot of Cambuskenneth during the 16th century. In destroying the abbey at Cambuskenneth, the earl had unwittingly sealed the fate of his lineage for years to come, for many of the predicted details of the curse, although cryptic when uttered, were to come shockingly true.

Remarkably, it was not unusual at that time for Scottish curses to predict suffering that would last for several generations, but this particular curse was very specific about certain matters. Most importantly, and typically for a curse of this kind, it was foretold that the Erskine family would become extinct – a fate which was the ultimate disaster for any hereditary aristocratic lineage. The curse elaborated further: before the family died out, all its estates and property would fall into the hands of strangers – again, this would have been a horrifying concept to a family of landed gentry.

At this point, it might have been expected that even the abbot's rage would have been satisfied, but the curse continued.

It predicted that a future Erskine would later live to see his home consumed by flames while his wife burned inside it and three of his children would never see the light of day. Moreover, adding further disgrace to the name of Erksine, the great hall of the family seat would be used to stable horses and a lowly weaver would work in the grand chamber of state. The curse was predicted to end only after all this had passed and an ash sapling had taken root at the top of the tower. Although the curse must have worried the Earl of Mar, he managed to live his entire life without seeing any of the predicted events come true and, on his deathbed, he must have reflected that the family had escaped from the abbot's wrathful utterings. In this, he was greatly mistaken.

This seems to have been a patient curse because it was a while before certain events began to show the truth behind the predictions. In 1715, a subsequent Earl of Mar declared his allegiance to James Stuart, the son of James VII of Scotland, who was known as 'the Old Pretender'. The earl led a failed Jacobite rebellion against the crown in an attempt to install James Stuart as king. He was defeated and, in retribution, the family were stripped of their land and titles – in this way, one part of the curse had come true. Whether the earl actually attributed this to the curse is unknown, as he might have merely viewed events as a punishment for his own actions. However, more of the predictions were to be borne out within a few generations.

Almost a century later, in 1801, it was John Francis Erskine who was unlucky enough to bear the brunt of the prophecy, and so pay the price for his ancestor's mistakes. To begin with, three of his children were born completely blind – thus, as the curse had foretold, they would 'never see the light of day'. Then Alloa Tower, all that remained of the family's former glory, was devastated by fire and Erskine's wife perished in the flames.

The main body of the curse had now come true and only the details were left to be completed. Sure enough, a troop of cavalry used the half-ruined hall as shelter for their horses while they were moving around the country. Subsequently, a homeless weaver took up residence in the ruins of the building and plied his trade in the nearby town. In around 1820 a small ash tree was seen to have taken root in the ruins of Alloa Tower. The curse had now been fulfilled in every detail.

Of all the questions that spring to mind in this case, the first revolves around the existence of the curse. Was it ever really uttered or could it have been made up after the events to explain and justify the demise of the Erskines and serve as a useful warning to other potentially rebellious landowners? Certainly, both historical fact and local folklore indicate that the curse was true, but there is always the possibility that, rather than having the ability to bring about such terrible events, the abbot was simply in possession of astonishing visionary powers.

Either possibility could apply in this case. Perhaps the abbot did have the power to seal the destiny of the Erskine family through a curse, or maybe his powers of divination were comparable to those of a prophet, although this would appear to be the only instance of such a prediction from the abbot. Whatever the truth of the matter, it seems that the mystical powers of the Abbot of Cambuskenneth were so great that they are remembered to this very day.

THE EVIL EYE

The 'evil eye' is one of the world's oldest superstitions, with many examples dating back to the time of the ancient Egyptians. It is also one of the most unusual curses, for it can be cast only by those who themselves possess the evil eye and, remarkably, it is usually cast unintentionally. The evil eye is able to place a curse on almost anything, from children and livestock to crops and property.

This curse seems to have resonance with a large sector of humanity as it is known all over the world. The Scottish term for it is *droch shuil*, the Italian *mal occhio*, the Arabic *ayin harsha* and the Hebrew *ayin horeh*. Belief in its power is most concentrated around the Mediterranean and Aegean seas, but extends into northern Europe, North Africa and the Middle East.

Those who possess the evil eye cannot simply acquire it – rather, they have to be born with it. Moreover, they may not have any malicious intent towards the object of the curse, but they can just be unlucky enough to spread misfortune with a simple glance.

Such a person was Pope Pius IX, who was said to possess the evil eye as catastrophe seemed to follow wherever he went.

Generally, however, the evil eye is possessed by women and, more specifically in Mediterranean countries, women with blue eyes. Those women unfortunate enough to fall into this category may be treated with fear and suspicion, or even as a witch in some societies, particularly if any form of misfortune befalls a community.

In many cultures, belief in the evil eye revolves around the perceived sin of envy, with the offending look depicted as being envious in its intent, although often accompanied by praise. Children brought up in such societies will be taught not to covet their neighbour's possessions or envy their success, for fear of the evil eye. The malevolent powers of the curse are believed to act upon those who possess the evil eye just as much as upon those on whom the curse is cast.

The evil eye seems to have been most powerful in matters connected with fertility, no doubt due to the fact that the lives of our ancestors were dominated by the fertility of the land. Thus, likely results of such a curse might be the illness of an infant, infertility, a failed crop or diseased livestock.

In an effort to counter such malevolence, therefore, fertility charms have commonly been worn. These charms, usually made out of horn or shell, were often representative of the sexual organs. If these were not available, various hand gestures could be made instead for the purposes of protection. Some of these gestures stay with us, although for most they have lost their ancient cultural connotations. For example, the middle finger that is extended from a clenched fist represents a penis, while the sign of the bull's head is a representation of the womb and fallopian tubes.

Even today, in the Mediterranean region, amulets and talismans are worn by many. The most common of these is a simple blue representation of the eye to return the stare to anyone who may issue the curse. Similarly, the eyes painted on the bows of fishing boats are intended to return the stare of the evil eye. Further east, in India, small mirrors and shiny surfaces are used to reflect the power of the evil eye back to whence it came. Strings of mirrors may be hung over or across doorways to protect the households within, and animals and vehicles are often adorned in this way.

Other attempts to neutralize the curse involve soiling whatever has just been praised or stared at. For example, in some cultures, it may be necessary to spit on one's child if it is thought that it has been cursed. In other cultures, boys may be dressed as girls, to prevent the envious evil eye being cast over any highly prized sons.

Many, particularly those in modern Western society, are sceptical of the existence of the evil eye, dismissing it as unscientific. Yet it is true to say that many people speak of picking up 'bad vibes' from another person, and would confess to feeling uncomfortable when confronted with a display of envy or jealousy. Perhaps it is possible for these emotions to manifest themselves in a physical way, the power of the curse depending in effect on the belief placed in it? Whatever the explanation – whether the curse is due to nothing more than the power of superstition or whether the evil eye really does have malevolent powers – there are certainly large numbers of people all over the world today who would not take kindly to being the object of the evil eye.

WEIRD NATURE

The sheer destructive potential of the weather, the oceans, earthquakes, volcanoes and floods is feared and respected all over the world. Just as awesome and marvellous are the wild creatures of the natural world, many of whom defy conventional thinking and baffle us with their complexity of design. Then there are the tales that have come down through the centuries about strange beasts – from the centaurs, cyclops and sea serpents of classical mythology to the strange animals sighted more recently, such as the Nandi Bear and Chupacabra.

New fields of study help to categorize these curious creatures, but they do not explain how or why they exist.

ROGUE WAVES

The destructive power of nature is perhaps at its most awe-inspiring when it occurs at sea. Lethal currents, whirlpools and, in particular, giant waves have all claimed many lives since man first started sailing the oceans and yet the source of some of these natural phenomena is yet to be fully explained.

Whereas a tsunami is a large wave that is known to have been caused by an underwater earthquake, such as happened in the Indian Ocean on 26 December 2004, it would appear that rogue waves can sometimes have no such origins. Appearing seemingly out of nowhere, these huge walls of water are terrifying in their power and wreak havoc on anything in their path. Mariners through the ages have spoken of these waves, but only recently has their existence been taken seriously.

Proof of the existence of the rogue wave was captured on camera in 1980 by a lucky survivor, who described seeing a great mass of water rising out of the sea and crashing down on the deck of his ship. This rare film image shows the wave in question towering above other waves in the water at that time. Calculations, using the known height of the ship's mast as a guide, estimate its height to have been as much as 20m (65ft) – this figure could, in fact, be increased to 30m (98m) because a huge trough of water usually precedes this type of wave, increasing its height substantially.

With the existence of these rogue waves now being increasingly acknowledged, some people believe that they could be the reason behind the many unexplained shipping losses that occur every year across the globe. Certainly, the ferocity of the water on striking a vessel is immense and is more than capable of destroying even the largest supertanker.

Furthermore, it appears that such giant waves are now being seen with growing regularity. While, according to the laws of mathematics, they should occur only once in a lifetime, naval records and radar images reveal that, over the course of a dozen years, a total of 466 waves were recorded as being significantly larger than the average size of other waves.

If, then, the rogue wave is now an accepted and ever-increasing phenomenon, what is believed to be its cause? Oceanographers remain baffled, as the three factors that are key to the development and size of normal waves – wind speed, the amount of open water and the length of time the wind blows across the sea – would seem not to apply in this case. If all waves are subject to the same conditions, why is it that one wave grows to a height of 34m (112ft), for example, while its neighbours might be only 10m (33ft) high?

One theory is that each rogue wave is the result of smaller waves joining together to form one huge mass of water. This could be caused when fast-flowing currents collide with opposing strong winds, slowing the waves down and allowing them to unite. As many rogue waves seem to occur in areas which are prone to exactly these conditions – such as the Gulf Stream, the Kuro Shio current to the south of Japan and around the legendary Cape Horn – this would appear to be a plausible explanation of some of the giant waves. However, it fails to shed any light on why such waves occur in waters where there are no fast-flowing currents.

Another explanation of this phenomenon is based on the chaos theory, a mathematical model that is applied more frequently to financial markets and the weather. With this rationale stating that tiny changes can lead to disproportionate results, it is possible that the slightest change in wave height, wind speed or direction could result in the creation of a colossal column of water. The mathematical equations that are being used to test this theory would appear to show that there might be some truth behind this hypothesis, although further tests will be necessary before any definitive conclusions can be drawn.

The fact remains that the cause of the rogue wave is still far from clear. Perhaps as the science of oceanography progresses, an explanation will present itself before long, giving human beings more understanding and awareness of the complexity of the world in which they live.

For now, however, it must be viewed as yet one more example of the unpredictable, inexplicable and devastatingly potent power of nature.

SOUNDS OF THE DEEP

The Earth's oceans are huge, unexplored underground kingdoms that have held mankind in their thrall for thousands of years. Today, these inaccessible areas remain as mysterious as the infinite expanses of space, although scientific advances have recently attempted to push back the boundaries of sub-aquatic understanding in order to cast some light on the black depths that cover our planet. This has produced several surprising results.

Scientists have established that one of the most effective methods of obtaining information about the underwater world is through the use of hydrophones. The origins of these underwater microphones can be traced back to the 1960s when they were utilized widely by the US Navy for the purpose of detecting the presence of Soviet submarines during the Cold War. Today, they have been found to be ideal for tracing, tracking and identifying the many sounds travelling through the water.

The hydrophones, which are in essence a kind of listening station, are positioned hundreds of metres below the ocean surface. At this depth, factors such as pressure and temperature trap the sound waves within a layer known as the depth sound channel and, as a consequence, the waves travel for many thousands of kilometres without suffering distortion.

When the sound waves come into contact with hydrophones they produce a spectrogram, a visual representation of sound. This can be analysed and compared to other, known, spectrogram patterns. Many ocean noises – such as those made by boats, submarines, whales and earth tremors, for example – occur frequently and are easily identifiable in this way, but there remains a large number of eerie echoes that evade explanation.

Most of these inexplicable noises occur at a low frequency and, therefore, have to be speeded up in order to be rendered audible to the human ear. While some sounds last for just a few minutes, others continue for years at a time, baffling researchers. Although underground volcanoes, icebergs and even enormous, undiscovered animals residing within the ocean depths have all been suggested as possible reasons for these peculiar sounds, the truth is still unknown.

One particularly mysterious noise picked up by hydrophone has been nicknamed 'Bloop'. While scientists suspect that this strange sound may emanate from an animal, since the spectrogram pattern showed the rapid variation in frequency characteristic of that produced by deep-sea creatures, there is one surprising factor in this case – the sheer volume of the noise.

The fact that the Bloop signal has been detected simultaneously by sensors located more than 4,800km (3000 miles) apart indicates that the noise produced is louder than that caused by any known animal. It has been suggested, therefore, that a giant squid, or some other type of undiscovered monster, could be roaming the depths of our oceans.

'Slowdown' is the name given to another signal that, again, raises more questions than it answers. The sound has been detected in the Pacific and Atlantic oceans several times a year since 1997, and continues to baffle experts all over the world. One leading scientist, Christopher Fox, observed that the noise, which he likened to that of an aircraft, was coming from a southerly direction and so may have originated in the Antarctic. In order to rule out any obvious, man-made explanation, he consulted the US Navy. His suspicions that the sound could have been caused by top-secret military equipment were, however, unfounded.

Another theory which is currently being studied is that the noise could be caused by the shifting of Antarctic ice at the South Pole. The spectrogram pattern produced by Slowdown is similar to that created in cases where friction is a factor, and might have arisen in this instance from the moving and shifting of huge masses of ice over land.

Many further tests will be necessary before the true origin of sounds such as Bloop and Slowdown can be confirmed. Whether they are indeed caused by the movements of mysterious alien creatures in the underwater depths, or whether there are other – purely geological – explanations, only time will tell.

GIANT SQUID

Horrifying myths and tales of giant squid have abounded in maritime circles for centuries. Fictional accounts of these creatures also exist, as, for example, in the pages of Herman Melville's famous novel *Moby Dick*. In truth, however, no one has ever actually seen a mature, live example of a giant squid. So does this monster of the deep belong merely to the realms of hearsay and fiction?

Scientists in Tasmania seem to think otherwise. Over the course of many years, the remains of huge sea beasts have been washed ashore, and the rotting residue of tentacled creatures has been discovered in the stomachs of whales. More recently, entire, smaller, juvenile specimens of these mysterious squid have been caught in deep-sea trawlers and brought to the Institute for Antarctic and Southern Ocean Studies in Tasmania for examination.

While little is known about most species of giant squid, experts are now much better informed about one type in particular – the Architeuthis or 'chief squid'. This tentacled sea monster was identified back in 1856 by a Danish researcher, and numerous reliable reports exist of the creature being washed up on shores around the world.

Despite all the horror stories about the creature's ferocity, however, recent studies have concluded that, despite its mammoth proportions, it is in fact very slow and relatively weak. It is thought to drift in the cold currents of the deep ocean rather than dart to attack its prey, and its pincer action is believed to be clumsy and feeble.

Numerous questions about this giant squid have yet to be answered. For example, how many different populations exist in the oceans of the world? How long do these creatures live? What do they eat and how often? How many years do they take to reach maturity?

As far as the last question is concerned, it seems reasonable to assume that, in view of the animal's great size, the growth period is considerable. However, studies of other squid have revealed otherwise, and some people actually believe that the total time taken to reach maturity could be as little as two years. This would make the creature one of the fastest growing beasts in the entire animal kingdom. Scientists are working hard to try to understand more about this enormous sea-dweller, and in so doing, hope to be able to shed light on other species of giant squid at the same time.

One species in which researchers are particularly interested is the Mesonychoteuthis or 'colossal squid'. Rumours about this variety of squid, which is thought to be even larger than Architeuthis, have been rife since 1925, when two tentacles were found in the stomach of a sperm whale. In 2004 the juvenile body of one of these creatures was caught off Antarctica. From studies carried out on the corpse, scientists have estimated that, had it reached maturity, it would have measured an astounding 15m (49ft) long.

It would seem that this species is responsible for all the terrifying tales about tentacled sea monsters. The colossal squid is physiologically different from its feeble, drifting cousin, the Architeuthis, being armed and deadly. It possesses a powerful, muscular fin, and has rotating hooks along its arms and tentacles. These factors would seem to correlate with the scars and sucker wounds found on the whales that share the freezing habitat of this creature, which is thought to be capable of striking with speed and lethal accuracy.

Many of these postulations are based on theory and on the studies of other species of squid. From the work carried out, scientists are of the opinion that there could be many other similar species of giant squid awaiting discovery in other parts of the world.

Perhaps future advances in deep sea technology will one day enable researchers to see one of these living creatures for themselves and so help to solve this maritime mystery.

Until then, it would seem that we possess more information about the long-extinct dinosaurs than about a number of the huge creatures that swim in our seas today.

A model of Architeuthis on display in the Natural History Museum in London.

LAKE MONSTERS

Many stories exist of serpent-like monsters living in the lakes and rivers of the world. Tales of creatures such as the Loch Ness Monster fascinate old and young alike, and continue to evoke curiosity and controversy in the scientific world.

Similar to 'Nessie' is 'Chessie', a long, dark, snake-like creature, which has been sighted on numerous occasions since the 19th century in the lake at Chesapeake Bay in the USA. Evidence of its existence has been captured on film by tourists, who continue to flock to the region in the hope of catching a glimpse of the mysterious serpent.

Further reports of Chessie emanate from respected members of the community, with witnesses including an FBI agent, ex-CIA officials and coast guards. Although a fairly accurate description of the animal has been achieved – around 10m (33ft) long, about one third of a metre (1ft) in diameter and with a humped brown back – no one has yet been able to establish exactly what kind of serpent it is. Some have suggested that it may even be an example of a dinosaur that has somehow survived to this day.

Another snake is rumoured to inhabit the waters of Lake Champlain, on the borders of New York and Vermont. Affectionately nicknamed 'Champ', the animal is said to have been seen in the region ever since 1609. Efforts have been made to try to establish the exact location of this first sighting, thought to be off the St Lawrence estuary. The serpent then appears to have migrated to Port Henry, where is was spotted first by settlers in 1819 and then by the sheriff of Clinton County in 1883.

With regular sightings now made in Lake Champlain, there is huge curiosity about this animal and many visit the area to try to see the creature for themselves. One such individual was Sandra Mansi, who was lucky enough to capture the animal on film. Experts have since analysed her photograph and denied that any kind of deception or forgery has taken place. Since then, there have also been unconfirmed sightings of a second, smaller, beast swimming alongside the larger animal. Could this be evidence that a mating pair are alive and well in the region?

A photograph of 'Champ' in the waters of Lake Champlain in the north-east of the United States of America.

Certainly, many people have no doubt of the existence of creatures such as Champ, but a number of questions still remain unanswered. Are these animals examples of the pleiosaur, a species of dinosaur long since believed to be extinct? If so, how many are there? How long do they live for? And, if they are indeed modern-day dinosaurs, how did they manage to survive when all the others perished?

Perhaps, in light of these numerous reports, the time has come for a reassessment of traditional theories concerning the extinction of the pleiosaur. With little information available on both the prehistoric and supposed modern-day version of this dinosaur, however, and the fact that sightings are fairly rare, scientists are faced with a daunting task. Unless a breakthrough discovery is made, it seems likely that the truth surrounding these dark creatures of the deep will continue to elude humankind.

THE BUNYIP

According to the Aboriginal dream of creation, deep in the heart of the Australian outback there lurks a mysterious creature known as the Bunyip. This beast is said to inhabit and defend lakes, swamps and billabongs, leaving its territory at night to venture into human dwellings to prey upon vulnerable women and children. Stories abound of its spine-chilling bellowing as it moves in search of its prey in and around the Australian waterways. But is this creature purely a fictional, symbolic warning about the very real dangers presented by the alligators that lurk in the inland waters of this vast continent? Or is there some truth behind the tales?

Among the Aborigines, there are varied descriptions of the Bunyip. Some say it is covered in feathers, others that it has scales like an alligator. Almost all describe the animal as having an equine tail, flippers and walrus-like tusks. These reports run counter, however, to the stories of the Bunyip related by the first Western settlers. Far from being a savage creature, these people describe the Bunyip as a kind of aquatic herbivore that lived in the waterways and peacefully grazed on the abundant grasses of the riverbanks and marshland.

These reports suggest that there were, in fact, two main species of Bunyip. The most often sighted of the two was the Dog-faced Bunyip, which, as its name suggests, possessed a canine face, a long, shaggy coat and small, wing-like flippers. The second species, the Long-necked Bunyip, apparently possessed a similar coat to the Dog-faced Bunyip, but with a longer neck, a horse-like mane, tusks and flippers.

There are numerous written and spoken accounts of encounters with Dog-faced Bunyips during the 19th and early-20th centuries. The creature was sighted in lakes, rivers and billabongs all over Australia and Tasmania. By contrast, reports of the rarer Long-necked Bunyip seem to be restricted to the state of New South Wales.

The sheer number and collaboratory nature of the stories seems to negate the possibility that these strange hybrid creatures belong purely to the realms of fantasy. But if they do exist in reality, what type of animal are they and where did they come from? And, most importantly from a conservational and cryptozoolological perspective, what has become of them?

Of the various theories in existence about the creature's origins, one in particular seems to have excited researchers, although many remain sceptical. The Bunyip bears a strong resemblance, both in its appearance and behaviour, to a supposedly extinct creature known as the Diprotodon, a large rhinoceros-sized herbivorous marsupial that roamed the land more than 10,000 years ago. Some experts believe that the Diprotodon was, like the Bunyip, equally at home on the land and in the water. Perhaps, then, in a land rich in marsupial diversity, the Diprotodon evolved over the course of thousands of years into a sort of marsupial hippo – the Bunyip? Although there are those who maintain that this might be possible, in general scientists have dismissed the notion that a few of these ancient animals may have somehow survived until the 20th century.

Another theory is that the Bunyip was, in fact, a seal and that the mystery is a simple case of repeated misidentification by inland locals who have never seen sea-dwelling seals. Similarly, it has been suggested that Bunyips might have been seals that migrated inland along the waterways, evolving to fit into their new surroundings by shedding their blubber and replacing it with thick fur.

These possibilities are also a matter of fierce debate, however. If the Bunyips were no more than seals, how could they have been observed grazing on land? Seals are aquatic mammals that feed on fish, not herbivorous grazers that are capable of living on land as well as in water. Moreover, the physical attributes of the Long-necked Bunyip do not match those of a seal.

There are many unanswered questions on the subject of the Bunyip, but it seems the truth will never be known. The Bunyip has not been seen for almost a century so if it really did exist, it may have perished as a result of environmental changes in the waterways and the effects of pollution.

The only place in which it would seem to live on is in the imaginations and traditions of the local people in the areas in which this enigmatic creature was seen.

NANDI BEARS

Of all Africa's unexplained animals, the Nandi bear is said to be the most ferocious and is consequently the most feared. It is renowned all over this huge continent, where it strikes terror into the hearts of both native people and Westerners alike. The nature of its existence is a mystery – is it really a bear, or could it be some other kind of animal? And how has it managed to avoid categorization by scientists?

There would certainly appear to be a strange, unidentified killer animal prowling around the villages on the east coast of Africa. Numerous eyewitness reports from both indigenous and Western inhabitants describe the beast as resembling a large hyena, being about the same size as a lion and having a dark, possibly reddish-brown, coat. It is said to be a nocturnal creature, and there are numerous reports of vicious attacks on humans.

Several accounts of this animal have been publicized in the Kenyan press, and one article, in particular, thrust it into the limelight. The report described the experiences of two of Kenya's most famous citizens, who were outside one moonlit night when they spotted what they believed, at first, to be a lioness. This initial identification was quickly proved to be inaccurate, however. As the animal became more visible, it could be seen to have a snout and a back which sloped down to its hind quarters, just like that of a bear. It also had the thick, dark fur and shuffling gait commonly associated with members of the bear family.

Although it is known, from the writings of Pliny and others, that bears did once roam this continent, according to official animal demographic statistics, there are no native, wild bears living in Africa today. Moreover, there is no evidence of the creature that might provide further, vital information. Although natives claim to have killed several of the beasts by setting fire to them and Westerners report having taken shots at the creature, the fact remains that no one has yet been able to make a positive identification.

It is known that one type of bear did once roam the continent, but this species is thought to have become extinct during the Paleolithic period. With so many factors – such as the animal's shape, behaviour, appearance and ability to stand on its hind legs – suggesting that this creature might be a type of bear, it has been asked whether some of this supposedly extinct species could have managed to survive, and evade detection by scientists.

Although this so-called Atlas bear matches the descriptions of the modern-day Nandi bear, the identification raises a number of significant problems.

Not least of these issues is the fact that fossil records of the Atlas bear have been found solely in northern Africa, whereas the Nandi bear is only located in the east of the country. It is unlikely that the Nandi bear is a different species of bear altogether for, apart from the fact that the Atlas bear is the only type known to have inhabited Africa, not one single fossil record of the Nandi has been discovered on this continent.

Perhaps, then, this mysterious beast is not a bear at all? Many people believe instead that it is some sort of huge, bloodthirsty hyena, which could either be a previously undiscovered species, or else a remnant from prehistoric times.

In support of this argument is the fact that archaeologists have found evidence of the existence on the continent of a short-faced hyena, similar in size to a lion which lived until the Paleolithic era.

Others suggest that the creature could be a chalicothere, a slope-back animal related to the horse, but having claws instead of hooves. Like the hyena, this species is also believed to have become extinct in the Paleolithic era. Although this description matches that of the Nandi bear, there is one crucial factor which makes the proposition less likely: the chalicothere, in common with all horses, was a herbivore, whereas the Nandi bear is known to be a vicious killer.

The Nandi tribe, from which the beast derives its most commonly used name, describe the bear as a primate, resembling a large baboon. Baboons are omnivores, known to make savage attacks on animals such as smaller monkeys and sheep, and are also able to stand on two feet. Differences in behaviour between the baboon and the mysterious animal – such as the fact that the baboon hunts in packs and is not nocturnal – have been noted, but can possibly be ascribed to the fact that the two creatures could have a slightly different genetic make-up.

On the evidence provided by the fossils of giant baboons and the description of the Nandi tribe, researchers are seriously considering the possibility that the Nandi bear could be some sort of hitherto unknown species of baboon. Alternatively, it might be a survivor from prehistoric times.

Until more thorough research is carried out, however, or a specimen has been caught, scientists and cryptozoologists are unable to verify exactly what kind of animal this is. Only once this is known can they start to solve the riddle of its origination.

ORANG-PENDEK

Tales of mysterious ape-like creatures are not uncommon. Indeed, the possible existence of animals such as the Yeti or Bigfoot has gripped the imagination of mankind for many years, and is an endless source of debate and intrigue. One creature that has been the subject of marked interest in recent years is the Orang-Pendek or 'little man'.

Accounts of this animal come from a range of sources, most notably from the local people of Sumatra, who have accepted it as a part of the diverse habitat in which they live. It is, they say, a shy creature that only kills small animals for food and has never attacked a human. It is therefore not regarded as a threat and is generally left alone by the natives.

The Orang-Pendek is described as short in stature, walking on its hind legs at a height of just 0.7m–1.5m (2ft4in to 5ft). Its pinkish-brown skin is covered with a coat of short, dark body hair and it has long, flowing hair around its face. Its arms, unlike those of most normal apes, are considerably shorter than its legs, and it appears more human than ape-like.

Many footprints have been discovered over the years, and these have been used as proof of the animal's existence. Although these prints are said to resemble those made by a child of around seven years old, they are in fact much broader than a human's and some accounts actually describe the feet as pointing backwards.

To add to the natives' accounts of the Orang-Pendek, a number of sightings of the creature by Western explorers have further corroborated the story. The first sighting of the Orang-Pendek by a Westerner occurred in 1910. The man described it as: 'a large creature, low on its feet, which ran like a man and was about to cross my path; it was very hairy and it was not an orangutan; but its face was not like an ordinary man's'. This description was echoed by that of a Dutch hunter 13 years later, who added that he felt unable to kill the beast because its physical appearance was so similar to that of a human being.

More recently, in the late 1980s, interest in the animal was reignited by the findings of the English travel writer, Deborah Matyr. Although initially sceptical that such a creature did in fact exist, after sighting it on several occasions and studying its footprints, she went on to become one of its most reliable and trusted witnesses.

Following the emergence of poor-quality photographic evidence of the creature a decade later, it was decided that conclusive evidence of the Orang-Pendek was needed; as the shadowy and blurred images that had been captured on film were deemed to be inadequate proof of its existence. Accordingly, a number of expeditions have set out lately to the Sumatran swamps to try to gather definite proof. The discovery of hair and faecal samples, casts of footprints and a clear and incontrovertible photo, for example, would not only prove once and for all that this creature exists, but would enable scientists to determine if it is an example of a species of ape previously unknown to zoologists.

Scientists are, alternatively, debating whether the Orang-Pendek might be linked in some way to the discovery, in a limestone cave on the Indonesian island of Flores, of a new species of miniature human. Evidence has been uncovered to show that these tiny people, nicknamed 'hobbits' on account of their diminutive stature, lived and hunted on the island 18,000 years ago. Perhaps this creature is not an ape at all, but, rather, an example of a sub-species of human being? It seems that further evidence will be needed before a definitive answer to the mystery of the Orang-Pendek is provided.

KONGAMATO

Although dinosaurs are known to have been extinct for thousands of years, a strange tale emanating from African natives in Zambia might, in fact, suggest otherwise. Over the centuries there have been numerous reports of ferocious flying reptiles that bear an uncanny resemblance to a supposedly extinct species of dinosaur called the pterosaur.

These claims have inspired such curiosity that, in 1932 Frank H. Welland ventured into the Jiundu swamps in the Mwinilunga district of western Zambia to investigate the story. The natives gave him detailed accounts of monstrous, reddish birds, with a wingspan of 1–2m (3ft 3in to 6ft 6in), long beaks full of teeth and leathery skin in place of feathers. They called these creatures 'kongamato', which translates as 'overwhelmer of boats', due to the fact that the huge birds would often overturn small vessels, attacking and sometimes killing the occupants. So terrified were the locals of the kongamato that it was thought that just one look at it would result in certain death. Welland wrote an account of the natives' descriptions in his book, *In Witchbound Africa*, which received great publicity for it also revealed that, when Welland showed the Zambians drawings of the prehistoric pterosaur, they unanimously and unhesitatingly agreed that these sketches identified precisely the creature they knew as the kongamato.

Many people were sceptical of these claims, and argued instead that the Zambian people had in fact obtained the description of the pterosaur from those natives who had worked on excavations in Tanzania where the fossilized bones of pterosaurs had been discovered some years earlier.

There are several problems with this theory, however. First, was it possible for descriptions of the dinosaur bones to have travelled from Tanzania to Zambia, a distance of 900km (560 miles)? Second, even if this had been the case, and the Zambians had heard about the skeletal structure of the pterosaur, how would they have known about the creature's leathery skin and lack of feathers? Finally, if the sightings were nothing more than the product of fervent imaginings, why was it that they did not come directly from the excavation site in Tanzania, rather than from as far away as Zambia?

Sightings of the mysterious creature continued, one story being told to the English newspaper correspondent, Mr G. Price, by a civil servant living in Africa. The expatriate recounted how he had met a native who had suffered an almost fatal wound to the chest while exploring the much-feared swampland. The man claimed that he had received his injury in an attack by a huge long-beaked bird.

Such stories were not limited to the inhabitants of the Zambian swamps, however. One account came from the famous zoologist and writer Ivan Sanderson who, in 1933, was leading an expedition to the Assumbo Mountains in the Cameroons on behalf of the British Museum. He described how, while out hunting one day, he had shot a fruit bat over the fast-flowing river. Wading out into the water to retrieve the fallen animal, Sanderson lost his balance and fell. Having regained his footing, he heard a warning yell from one of his colleagues and to his horror saw a monstrous black creature bearing down upon him from the sky at great speed.

Sanderson ducked into the river to escape the huge bird and then made for the riverbank. At this point, the creature renewed its attack, diving down on him again and both he and his companion threw themselves on the ground, conscious only of the sound of the beating of the creature's powerful wings. Fortunately, the animal then flew off into the night, leaving the two men to return to the safety of their camp. Here, they related their story to the natives, asking them if they knew what their attacker might have been. The locals fled in terror without answering the question.

Sanderson reflected on what he had seen – fortunately, he had had sufficient time to note the physical appearance of the creature and, due to his zoological expertise, was able to give a precise description of the animal. He described it as having been about the size of an eagle, with a semicircle of sharp white teeth in its lower jaw. This report matched not only those of other sightings, but also corresponded with what is known of the pterosaur. Sanderson also remarked that the beast, like the pterosaur, resembled a bat. However, he discounted the possibility that it was only a fruit bat on the basis that these creatures are not known to attack humans.

Some years later, in 1942, similar stories from other areas in Africa, such as Mount Kilimanjaro and Mount Kenya, were related to the author, Captain C. Pitman. They described the existence of a large bat-like bird, which produced tracks suggesting that it had a large tail that dragged along the ground behind the creature.

In his book *A Game Warden Takes Stock*, Captain Pitman went on to describe how the animals were alleged to feed on rotting human flesh if corpses were not buried to a sufficient depth. Further accounts of the birds were contained in another publication, *Old Fourlegs*, in which fossil expert Dr J. L. B. Smith described 'flying dragons' in the region of Mount Kilimanjaro.

Today the sightings continue in remote areas of Africa. In 1998, a Kenyan exchange student, Steve Romando-Menya, declared that the existence of the kongamato is common knowledge among the bush dwellers in his country. Moreover, all witnesses, when asked to draw what they have seen, are repeatedly reported to draw a pterosaur.

What are these mysterious creatures? Sceptics claim that it is impossible for the prehistoric pterosaur to be in existence today, and yet the number of confirmed reports from reliable sources would seem to indicate otherwise. The controversy and debate continue to this day.

MOKELE-MBEMBE

For hundreds of years, natives living in the depths of the African jungle have spoken of a large, water-dwelling beast unfamiliar to Western science. It is known by a variety of names and has been sighted by many of the local population, but has yet to be positively identified or photographed by anybody from outside the area. So does it really exist and, if so, what type of creature is it?

Explorers travelling across the vast continent of Africa in the 1900s were told many tales about strange beasts, most of which are now as familiar to us as normal domestic pets. Among these stories were repeated claims by tribesmen that they shared their land with swamp-dwelling creatures the size of an elephant and possessing a long neck and tail. Evidence of the animals could be seen in their rounded tracks, containing three claw marks, on the banks of the local rivers.

In 1932, a cryptozoologist, Ivan Sanderson, discovered animal tracks resembling those of the hippopotamus in an area in which no such animals lived. On discussing his find with the native people, he was told that the animal responsible for making such unusual footprints was known as the mbulu-eM'bembe. Later that day, he caught sight of a creature, in the water, that appeared to be larger than a hippopotamus, but it disappeared under the surface before he had the chance to make a closer inspection.

The same animal is known to the pigmy tribes of the Likouala region of the Republic of Congo. They call the creature Mokele-mbembe, which means 'rainbow', 'one that stops the flow of rivers' or 'monstrous animal', depending on who is using the term. They describe the animals, which must seem particularly huge to them given their diminutive stature, as being hairless vegetarians, with reddish-brown or grey skin and a neck that is more than 3m (10ft) in length. Interestingly, their description of the animals' tracks is the same as that given by Ivan Sanderson.

Since 1932, many more scientists and explorers have visited these areas in the hope of catching a glimpse of the elusive monster. Unfortunately, none of them has ever witnessed anything, although, according to natives,

Could Mokele-mbembe be a relative of this long-dead dinosaur?

a creature with a long neck and tail was killed near Lake Tele in 1959. If this mysterious creature does exist, what kind of animal is it? Eyewitness reports would seem to suggest that the animal strongly resembles a sauropod dinosaur. This theory was put to the test by James Powell, an American explorer, who visited the area with the aim of solving the mystery. On showing a picture of a sauropod to the many tribes who said they had seen the animal, all instantly confirmed that the Mokele-mbembe was indeed a sauropod.

Dinosaurs are believed to have become extinct many millions of years ago, so how could the sauropod have survived when the rest of these prehistoric creatures perished? One explanation for their continuing existence might be the fact that their remote habitat is more similar than anywhere else on the planet to the environment in which the original sauropod would have lived. It has also been suggested that they owe their survival to their innate shyness, which has kept them hidden from curious, prying and potentially harmful eyes.

Whatever the nature of these enigmatic beasts, they are undoubtedly central to the debate about cryptozoology. If indeed they do exist, and could be proved to do so, this would overturn centuries of thought about the natural history of our planet and our own evolution.

CHUPACABRA

From the southern states of the USA and Central and Southern America comes the strange story of a beast that defies explanation. This creature, known as Chupacabra, or the 'goat sucker', is rumoured to stalk the streets, killing livestock and terrorizing entire neighbourhoods. Does this animal really exist, and if so, what are its origins?

Although reports of the creature's existence date back to the 1970s, it was given the name Chupacabra following the mysterious deaths of a number of animals, primarily goats, in Puerto Rico in the 1990s. Those farmers who had lost livestock were perplexed by the nature of the killings, which were totally different from those of any other predator. The killer had not attempted to eat the flesh of its victim, nor did it drag the carcass away for consumption at a later date. In fact, the only clue as to the cause of death was the existence of a puncture wound on the animal's neck and it was found that the blood had been drained from its body.

Word of the gruesome nature of this vampiric creature spread quickly. According to *UFO* magazine, more than 2,000 animal mutilations in just two years – from Miami and Texas to Chile, Mexico and Puerto Rico – were blamed on the elusive killer. Although there is no photographic evidence of the goat-sucker, there have apparently been numerous sightings of the animal, although descriptions vary wildly.

Some witnesses claim that the goat sucker is a small, flying hybrid – an alien-type creature crossed with a dinosaur, with quills down its back and no tail. Some describe it as a cross between an ape, a human and a bird, just over a metre in height, with glowing red eyes, grey skin, hairy arms, fangs and a wingspan of more than 2m (6ft 7in). Some assert that it resembles a panther, with a long tongue and fangs. Others state that it is a small creature that hops along the ground, leaving a stinking trail of sulphuric acid behind it.

The debate concerning the creature's appearance is only one of a number of questions to surround the Chupacabra. Of more importance to many is the conundrum of its origins – just where does it come from, and why is it here?

Of the many theories that abound, three have a particularly strong following. Some believe that the beast might be a species of dinosaur, previously unknown to man, that has managed to survive to this day. Some think that it is a type of extra-terrestrial pet, abandoned by aliens during an expedition to this planet. There are others who assume that this 'Anomalous Biological Entity' (as creatures such as the Chupacabra are known by UFO enthusiasts) is the consequence of a disastrous genetic experiment that endeavoured to combine the genes of an alien with those of an earthly animal.

Whether such an experiment was performed by humans or aliens is a matter of much controversy, which has been further fuelled by the results of blood analysis from a creature believed to be a dead Chupacabra. This report states that the animal's blood is unlike that of any known earthly animal. Whether this is due to the advanced scientific nature of any genetic manipulation that might have taken place or to the fact that the animal is an extra-terrestrial being is not clear. The identity of this curious beast remains shrouded in mystery. Whether it is an unknown species of dinosaur, a creature of alien origin or indeed a specimen of advanced genetic engineering is a matter that may never be fully resolved, although no doubt the speculation will continue until a definitive answer is found.

THE JERSEY DEVIL

The malevolent figure of the devil is a symbol of evil that is present in almost every society and religion in the world. Throughout the ages, mankind has sought an answer to the question of its existence – is it a purely mythical creature, or could it be grounded in reality? Sightings of a terrifying otherworldly creature in New Jersey may clarify some of this uncertainty.

Numerous stories exist about the origins of the beast, although none of these versions has been conclusively proven. The tales contain slight variations in terms of the date, location, parentage and physical appearance of the demon, but there are, interestingly, some common themes running through the tales. The most obvious of these is the occurrence of the word 'Leeds' in separate accounts.

One of the most popular legends attributes the birth of the demon to a Mrs Shrouds of Leeds Point, who apparently made an ominous vow that if she ever became pregnant again, she desired the child to be a devil. Imagine her horror when she conceived shortly afterwards. When the boy was born, he was afflicted with terrible deformities, so she kept the child at home, away from prying eyes. The story relates how, one day, the infant started to flap his arms, which suddenly transformed themselves into a bat's wings. He then flew out of the open window into the night, never to be seen again.

Another account tells of a young girl living in Leeds Point who fell in love with an English soldier and became pregnant. Soon after this, he broke her heart by leaving the area with his division. The girl was shunned and cursed by the community, and nine months later gave birth to the devil.

While opinion is divided about the details of the conception and birth of the devil, there are no arguments about the sightings. The strange being is said to have been seen by more than 2,000 people over the last 260 years, causing havoc in the small towns surrounding the New Jersey Pine Barrens. Factories and schools have closed down as a result and whole communities have been consumed by fear. Sightings of the creature have taken place primarily in three distinct time periods – prior to 1909, during the week of

16–23 January 1909, and after 1909 – and they are corroborated by written eyewitness accounts.

Prior to 1909, encounters with the supernatural beast were frequent. Among those who saw the devil were Joseph Bonaparte (brother of Napoleon and former king of Spain) and the naval figure, Commodore Stephen Decatur, who actually shot the flying creature with a cannon ball. Amazingly, however, this action caused it no visible harm.

From 1840-41 there were numerous reports of farm animals being killed by an unknown creature that had an eerie, alien scream and left strange tracks behind it.

As the century progressed, these reports became more frequent, and many domestic animals were seen being carried off by a mysterious predator. On a visit to the region, the mayor of New York noted that the local residents seemed terrified, and refused to leave their homes after dark.

Then, in one highly dramatic week, there was the most concentrated number of sightings to date. From 16–23 January 1909, the devil was seen by more than 1,000 people and its tracks were evident all over South Jersey and Philadelphia. Although there was a slight variation in the descriptions given of the creature that week, all said that it was able to fly, that it had a spine-chilling, otherworldly scream, and left strange prints in the snow. Trappers were mystified by the prints, which they had apparently never seen before, and were astonished to see that the trail went over rooftops and up trees. Attempts at hunting the animal were further thwarted by the fact that the tracker dogs refused to go near the prints.

During that week, the most prolonged close sighting of the beast occurred in Gloucester, outside the house belonging to Mr and Mrs Evans. The couple observed the creature for ten minutes, and reported that it had a head like a collie dog, but the face of a horse. It was about 1m (3ft 3in)in height, with a long neck and a large wingspan. It walked on its hind legs, which were similar to those of a crane, but had hooves instead of claws. The strange hybrid quality of this animal bears similarities to other reports, which describe it as a strange bird with glowing eyes and a horse's head.

Sightings of the animal both in the air and on the ground continued throughout the week, striking fear into the heart of the community and evoking intense speculation. Many attempts were made to capture or kill the creature, but it managed to escape every time.

Since 1909, the sightings have continued, although to a lesser extent. This decline could be attributed to a more cynical society, in which people are reluctant to make known their stories for fear of ridicule.

A number of theories have been put forward to explain the creature. Some believe that it is a scrowfoot duck, although this does not accord with the size of the animal as reported by witnesses. Others think it is a sand crane, which has not been seen in the region for many years. While similarities exist between the size and some of the behavioural patterns of this animal and accounts of the demonic creature, there is still no explanation for the horse's head, bat's wings, hooves or glowing eyes, or, for that matter, for the attacks on domestic animals.

A scientific theory that has been put forward is that the devil may be a relic from the Jurassic period, such as a pterodactyl, that has somehow managed to survive since that period, hiding away underground or in a cave. While this is perhaps possible, the description of the creature does not match that of any dinosaur from this era in history.

More superstitious explanations are based on the notion that the creature is the embodiment of evil and a harbinger of bad tidings or impending conflict. The dates of some of the sightings appear to support this idea, with reports being recorded shortly before the Civil War, the Spanish American War, the First and Second World Wars and the Vietnam War.

Whatever the origin and purpose of this intriguing being, it seems that its existence is beyond question. The frequency, reliability and time span of the sightings rule out the possibility that it is merely a creature of myth, or that events surrounding its appearance are all an elaborate hoax. Moreover, it looks likely that the creature is here to stay.

Speculation continues in New Jersey about the possible circumstances of the next sighting.

SKINWALKERS

The state of Utah is home to numerous supernatural occurrences and strange beings. Of these, the so-called 'skinwalker', or 'Wendigo', is perhaps the most terrifying and the question of its existence continues to mystify and bewilder the inhabitants of this part of the USA.

According to Native American legend, the skinwalkers are a band of shape-shifting Navajo witches that roam the countryside terrorizing humans and animals alike. They can take on the form of any animal at any given moment, acquiring the inherent strengths and attributes of that particular creature while at the same time retaining their innate human cunning.

This ability to maintain human intelligence while gaining the sensory or speed advantages of a specific animal renders the skinwalker a truly awe-inspiring and formidable foe. In addition to the possession of everyday human knowledge, these witches are blessed with those powers that lie outside the realms of common wisdom. So a witch in the guise of a coyote will have amazing agility, strength and speed, combined with the dark powers of mind control and a knowledge of curses and other occult crafts.

Native tradition relates that the skinwalkers have no choice about their metamorphoses, and that each change causes them much pain and torment. Perhaps it is for this reason that they show such ferocity towards the creatures around them, jealous of their ability to maintain a fixed identity and so remain exempt from the perpetual torment of mutability.

As a result of the witches' constantly changing identity, very little is known about their origins or habits. Many believe that they are linked to a region called 'Skinwalker Ridge' which, according to extra-terrestrial enthusiasts, is close to a region of intense UFO activity and which Native Americans studiously avoid. Could this region be a portal to another dimension from which the shape-shifters originate? Some people think so.

What is known about these eerie beings has been gleaned from the many reports in existence. Sightings by Navajo Indians tell of the creature's glowing yellow eyes and ability to strike terror into even the bravest observer. Encounters are not resticted to the Navajos, however, as the events of 1983 show. The isolated stretch of Route 163 that runs through the heart of the Monument Valley Navajo Tribal Park, although stunningly beautiful, is renowned for being the site of strange, otherworldly activities and local people warn outsiders that they should never venture into the region at night.

On this particular occasion, four members of a family were returning home from Wyoming, where they had been visiting friends. The most direct route was along Route 163, and having driven along this road without incident on the outward journey, they thought nothing of taking this course again on the way home.

The family reported that, on this pitch-black, moonless summer's evening, they had been driving for several hours without seeing another human being. They were making steady progress when the father who was driving mentioned that they were no longer alone. Looking behind them, the whole family saw headlights some distance behind the car.

They continued on their journey, keeping the distant lights in their sights and afterwards said that they felt slightly comforted in the knowledge that there would be help at hand should their vehicle break down.

Suddenly, however, the lights from the other car disappeared. Disquieted by this fact, the daughter, Frances, asked her parents whether they should go back to see if the occupants of the vehicle required any assistance.

Her father was anxious not to prolong their journey, however, and instead insisted that they should keep going. Frances afterwards said that it was at this time that the atmosphere in and around the car changed ominously. Her sixth sense was proved to be justified a few minutes later. As they slowed to round a sharp bend in the road, the father saw something ahead on the road. Crying out in surprise, he struggled to maintain control of the car and it almost veered off the road.

The rest of the family, alarmed by the evident panic in his voice, pushed down the locks and held fast on to the door handles, even though at this point they had no idea what had caused him to yell out. Everything became all too clear when he slammed on the brakes to prevent the vehicle from careering over the edge of a steep drop. Leaping towards their vehicle was a creature unlike any the family had ever seen before. Although dressed in a man's clothing, the monstrous being could not be described, by any stretch of the imagination, as a normal human.

Describing the course of events later to a Navajo friend, Frances recalled that the beast was black and very hairy, with long arms which clung on to the side of the car, and an anguished face that stared in at them for a few seconds before they sped away along the road.

Having reached the relative civilization of the nearest town, the family felt able to discuss the terrifying sight that they had recently witnessed. Shaken by what had happened, they were keen to see some evidence that their imagination had not been responsible for the strange events, and so made a thorough inspection of the car. Incredibly, there was not one single mark or print to be seen in the thick dust that had inevitably accumulated on the vehicle during its long journey. Neither was there any sign in the town of the vehicle that had been following them until the time of its sudden disappearance.

Although reports of encounters with the skinwalkers in one form or another are not uncommon among the Navajo, what is notable about this occurrence is that this family was not of Native American origin.

Among the many questions to be raised by these bizarre happenings are the following: why were these people chosen by the strange supernatural beings? And what did they want from them?

These curious shape-shifting witches have aroused great debate in this part of the USA and all over the world. Other beings that are said to possess a similar mutability are the werewolves of European renown, which also have the same ability to inspire awe and terror in the unlucky observer.

The provenance and purpose of these malevolent beings remains a matter of intense controversy and, until more evidence comes to light, the mystery will continue.

UFOS

There is a strong body of belief that intelligent and highly developed life already exists within the universe. Many sightings of UFOs are alleged to have taken place all over the world, but the greatest concentration comes from the USA, currently the most technologically advanced nation on Earth. Could the sightings represent a typically modern fear of technological destruction or are they, rather, based on something more grounded in reality? Since the first UFO was glimpsed, the number of sightings has increased dramatically, so could our own tentative steps into the solar system and the wider universe have come to the attention of other, more intelligent, species?

ALIEN ABDUCTIONS

Since the Second World War, alien encounters appear to be among the most commonly experienced forms of paranormal contact and prominent among these are reported abductions. Many people have come forward to offer their own individual accounts of extra-terrestrial activity, generating huge controversy over the alien hypothesis. Do such beings really exist or are there other explanations for these events?

Interestingly, the many different accounts of alien abductions would seem to share a number of basic similarities, lending credence to the reports. A large number of the abductees have described how they have been transported from their normal surroundings to the confines of an alien craft by means of a bright light, which has trapped them within its beam.

Once with the aliens, they have then been subjected to some form of physical experimentation, and many speak of telepathic communication with their temporary alien hosts. Whereas some individuals have related their story as being particularly harrowing, with their responses to pain and other more unusual stimuli being tested, others have reported a great feeling of empathy and understanding with their captors. A common feeling is that the aliens have come to Earth to intervene in its issues and conflicts and thus prevent mankind from bringing about its own demise.

In some more sinister accounts, however, abductees have described how small devices were implanted into them, often being placed into the brain through the nose and mouth. Others have claimed that their reproductive organs have been harvested, leading to notions of a hybrid alien/human race and even to some of the more bizarre conspiracy theories regarding alien infiltration among the more powerful governments on Earth.

Although the abductees' experiences seem to share some fundamental common ground, adding credence to the alien theory, there are nevertheless some factors that suggest otherwise.

Firstly, most of the abductees were alone at the time of the incident, meaning that it is extremely difficult for their stories to be corroborated.

Secondly, rather than the reporting of a uniformity of alien appearance,

The site of an alleged UFO encounter. The bright light is a common feature of many abduction accounts.

many different types of extra-terrestrial being have allegedly been encountered. Although the most commonly described alien is the 'Grey' – the small grey being with a large head and huge eyes – countless other shapes, sizes and colours of extra-terrestrial have been observed, often supported by varying accounts of the places from where the aliens have allegedly originated.

It has been pointed out that, although it might be possible for an intelligent alien race to contact Earth, the chances of several different alien

227

species performing the same kind of abduction are very remote indeed.

In support of this is the lack of any physical evidence being reported, other than the alleged alien autopsy film footage from the mysterious Roswell incident.

Many sceptics have proclaimed that the alien abduction phenomenon is little more than a modern folk tale. Our ancient folklore contains many stories of abductions by strange mythical creatures, such as fairies or goblins, some of which bear striking similarities to the accounts of alien abductions. For example, both tend to involve the distortion of time, during which abductees feel as if they have been absent for several hours, and yet are returned to their former surroundings only a few minutes after they left.

It has been pointed out that the alien might just be an updated version of these mystical beings, borne out of both the human fascination with superstition and fantasy and mankind's technological advancement. Certainly, prior to the advent of the space age, there was very little reported alien activity on Earth.

It has also been suggested that alien abductions are not actually the result of an exterior force, but instead derive from the collective human subconscious. This does not make the experiences any less mysterious, but it might explain the many discrepancies between the stories that are told, such as the profound differences between the alien races encountered. If these journeys do not actually take place in the physical reality, but rather occur in an 'inner space', what might this involve?

The accounts of abductees' experiences have much in common with the reports of those individuals who have undergone a profound hallucinatory trance. Just as abductees describe instances of telepathic communication with their alien captors, so do those who are gifted with the ability to communicate with the spirit world speak of visionary experiences with other beings.

Similarities abound between the tales of alien abductions and the shaman, for example. The shaman would, often as a result of poisons or hallucinogens, enter a deep trance-like state, leaving the confines of the

Earth and entering the spirit world. Here, they would converse with the non-human spirits who possessed remarkable powers such as flight and telepathy. The experience might frequently involve some kind of physical inspection and sometimes the shaman would be cut open and their organs replaced with new ones to allow them greater powers.

The experiences of the shaman and other gifted individuals would have been explained by past cultures in terms of the elemental spirits and mythical creatures that held cultural currency at the time. If these events were to be transposed into our modern culture, then it is likely that, on returning from such a revelatory experience, the human mind would struggle to find terms to explain what had occurred. Perhaps the easiest way to describe events would be in terms of an alien encounter rather than a spiritual one. This argument has been gaining in popularity among those sceptical of the idea of intelligent alien intervention.

If it is true that these modern abductees are actually venturing on more of a psychic journey than a paranormal one, there are still many questions to be answered. Why would this kind of experience happen spontaneously to people when they are on their own? What is the meaning of these events?

It could be that these experiences constitute a journey into mankind's spiritual past and into the collective subconscious, after which the individual concerned feels somehow altered.

Many people have explained that after their abduction they remain in some kind of contact with the aliens they encountered, who frequently offer advice for mankind. Maybe, rather than an alien communication, these individuals are instead conversing with the spirit guides in the collective human consciousness, which voice themselves through a few susceptible people. In our modern technological and spiritually fractured world, it is possible that we have lost some essential connection with the deeper facets of the human mind, and it is this that is surfacing in these encounters.

Whether the answer to the mystery lies, as some believe, in outer space, or within the deep recesses of the complex human brain is unknown. Certainly, the reports of alien encounters are so widespread that they should not be dismissed, but then again, we should not underestimate the psychic abilities of our own intelligent species.

As we stand on the threshold of a new age of space exploration and development, perhaps these questions will be answered sooner than we imagine. Will we like what we hear?

SIGHTINGS

One of the most intriguing mysteries surrounding the study of Unidentified Flying Objects (UFOs) is the question of a conspiracy theory. For many years, it has been suggested that the authorities might have a vested interest in preventing the public from learning the truth about attempted alien contact. Nothing has fuelled this idea more than the various accounts of alien crash sites.

Compared with the frequency of claims of abduction, which are difficult to verify, there have been very few reported instances of alien landings or crashes, incidents that might provide hard evidence to support the existence of UFOs. On the few occasions in which a group of people have all claimed to see a UFO make a landfall, any potential trace of the landings has mysteriously disappeared, leading the witnesses to accuse government organizations of a cover-up.

Many of these instances are reasonably well known, as a result of the popularity of some of these accusations among Western media. Perhaps the most famous of these occurred in 1908, when a remarkable explosion took place in Tunguska, Russia. Amidst all the speculation that took place as to the nature of the blast, one hypothesis suggested the possibility of an alien spacecraft crashing into the forest.

Many believed in the likelihood of this theory due to the incredible force of the explosion, which is estimated to have been equivalent to that inflicted by a 40-megaton nuclear weapon. The blast was so powerful that the forest, within a radius of 30km (19 miles), was destroyed and the results were felt and witnessed more than 300km (190 miles) away.

What could have caused such an explosion? It took place in one of the poorest, most remote regions of Russia, and occurred around 40 years before the development of nuclear weaponry. The men chosen to investigate the mystery took accounts from eyewitnesses in the area, who described a colossal ball of flame descending from the skies and then exploding. Scientists were forced to conclude that the matter that had caused the explosion must have originated from space, as nothing on Earth at that time was capable of generating such a forceful blast.

We are therefore presented with two possibilities. If the explosion was caused by an extra-terrestrial body, this could either have been a meteor, or else some kind of spacecraft. Strangely, an examination of the entire site yielded no fragments of rock or anything else of note, meaning that whatever had caused the impact had either completely vapourized in the atmosphere from the explosion, or else had been physically removed from the site. As the area was not formally inspected until 1927, almost two decades after the event, there is plenty of room for speculation in either direction.

Similarly, another suspected UFO crash site that is surprisingly devoid of any evidence is located near the town of Roswell in New Mexico, USA. Here, in 1947, several unconnected people witnessed an unknown craft crashing into the desert. Following this, the authorities made an official announcement to the effect that a UFO crash had taken place. This is thought to be the only example of such a declaration. However, shortly afterwards, the statement was retracted, derided as being spurious and the official account was changed to register the fact that it was an advanced experimental weather balloon that had crashed.

This report conflicted with the personal accounts of several witnesses, who claimed not only that they had discovered the wreckage of the extra-terrestrial craft, but also that they had seen the corpses of alien beings. These stories are corroborated by the initial report from the armed forces and would also seem to be backed up by the discovery in 1995 of film footage purporting to come from the autopsy of the alien following the alleged crash. Many have interpreted the peculiar events at the Roswell crash site as a sign both of the existence of aliens and a conspiracy of concealment by the government.

Some years later, in 1974, a similar incident took place in the British Isles, in what has been referred to as the 'British Roswell'. Several people living near the village of Llandrillo in Clwyd, Wales, reported seeing strange flying orbs in the skies and hearing a subsequent crash. Could a UFO landing have taken place in the sparsely populated Welsh countryside?

One account, given by a retired soldier using the pseudonym of James Prescott because of his desire for anonymity, claims that the RAF had recovered from the site an alien spacecraft that contained the bodies of two creatures. These alien corpses were apparently taken under a large armed guard to the UK's controversial government research facility at Porton Down.

Other witnesses describe a remarkably fast response to the crash – given the remoteness of the area – from the emergency services, and a suspiciously high military presence. Welsh farmer Huw Lloyd, who was 14 years old when the event happened, recalls it vividly.

He explained that he saw a large object streak to the ground leaving a flaming trail behind it. He said that the object was glowing, and that it emitted a flashing blue light.

All government papers relating to the incident and the subsequent military operation have remained classified to this day and the authorities refuse to comment on the issue. To some, this response can be taken as an almost tacit acceptance of the existence of UFOs, but without any physical evidence available, the truth of the actual events will continue to be a mystery.

The fact remains that, although there are those who fervently support the claims made in many of these eyewitness accounts, the vast majority of people are unwilling to believe in the existence of UFOs without the provision of some real proof. As no such evidence has yet come to light, it might indeed suggest that the truth of the matter has been concealed from the public by the authorities as part of a wider international conspiracy.

Until now, most of these suspected alien crash landings have occurred in relatively isolated areas. If such an event were to take place in a densely populated place such as a city, the results would be very different indeed. Without such a public event, however, it is unlikely that the debate on UFOs will alter from the polarized state in which it exists today. We can only hope that, if we do ever encounter intelligent alien life, it turns out to be benign.

GREYS

The question of whether alien life forms exist has permeated society for many years. When considering the appearance and behaviour of such extra-terrestrial beings, it is perhaps the image of the 'Grey' alien that initially springs to mind. These creatures, with small bodies, thin, spindly limbs and oversized heads, are instantly recognizable to anyone familiar with popular Western culture and indeed the image of the Grey alien has probably superseded the original 1950s flying saucer as an iconic representation of the extra-terrestrial world. Although those claiming to have been in contact with aliens describe a huge array of different species, sightings of the Greys outnumber those of any other suggested alien species.

In terms of their physical appearance, the Greys are described as being smaller than adult humans, about 1m (3ft 3in) in height, and almost childlike in their proportions. Their heads are much larger than those of humans, which seems to point towards the much higher level of intelligence with which they are credited. They have no hair whatsoever, but instead have a kind of pasty, grey skin that resembles rubber. It is this colouring that gives rise to their name. Their bodies are strangely flexible, and the fact that there are no visible joints in the arms or legs suggests that they are not skeletal creatures. From the descriptions given by their numerous abductees and witnesses, we have gleaned more information about the

Greys' characteristics. Although they are said to have mouths, these are small and slit-like and are not their primary means of communication. Rather, they are believed to communicate with one another through a form of telepathy that is thought to be directed through their eyes. These eyes, which are elongated rather than round, are much larger than those of human beings and are jet black throughout, with no distinction of iris or pupil.

This image of the Greys matches, in many respects, theories regarding the future evolutionary development of humans. The Greys are essentially humanoid, but their brainpower appears to have evolved to a significant extent, revealed by the fact that the size of their heads is so disproportionate to that of their bodies – in fact, their bodies seem to have atrophied over time. Some believe that human physiology will follow this course when the more physical demands of our environment are superseded by the mental ones – and thefore a greater brain capacity.

The alien corpses that were displayed in the infamous 'Roswell autopsy tapes' accord with the descriptions of these creatures, and are cited as near-incontrovertible evidence by believers in the existence of aliens. This apparent evidence is also used to further the claims of a government conspiracy over, and even a complicity with, the aliens. This is a particularly sinister suggestion as, of all the alien species to have been credited with abducting people, the Greys behave in a particularly unpleasant way to their abductees.

The curiosity shown by these aliens towards the human race appears to know no boundaries, and their alleged experiments can be both violent and painful. Part of the reason for the Greys' apparent lack of understanding or concern for human pain or emotion, and indeed their curiosity over it, arises from the fact that they have a form of gestalt consciousness. In other words, they operate with a hive-like mentality, rather than existing as separately defined individuals.

The extent of knowledge we possess on the subject of the Greys is remarkable given the fact that their existence has yet to be scientifically proven. Some of the most detailed information about the aliens' activities has come from supposed abductees. These individuals have given vivid descriptions of their encounters, and have answered many questions about the extra-terrestrial life forms, although doubts have also been raised over the veracity of their stories.

One of the most famous cases of alien abduction, that of the couple Betty and Barney Hill, has revealed some interesting facts about the origins of the Greys.

Following their claims of being abducted while returning from a holiday in Canada, the couple were placed under hypnosis for the purposes of divining any hidden information that they may have gleaned during their experiences. Betty recounted her discussions with the aliens as to the whereabouts of their origins in space, and while still under hypnosis she drew a map of the stars to demonstrate what she had been told.

Studies of this map appeared to show that it was a correct depiction of the star system Zeta Reticuli, a pair of stars that exist 37–38 light years away from Earth. Since this discovery, many have come to believe that Zeta Reticuli is the home of the Greys. Although no planets have yet been discovered orbiting the star system, the science of finding planets is still in its relative infancy and it is believed to be possible that some planets may be discovered there at a later date.

The frequency and similarity of the reports of abductions or visitations by the Greys has led many to reflect that they are both the most credible and the most likely of all our possible extra-terrestrial visitors. Scientific experiments, however, would seem to suggest otherwise, indicating that the prominence of the image of the Greys in Western culture has had an influence on the accounts of alleged abductees. Maybe these aliens are not actually as prevalent a species of extra-terrestrial as has been assumed to be the case.

In the experiments, the test subjects comprised individuals who had not claimed any previous contact with aliens; they were placed under hypnosis, and given a brief account of an alien encounter that they were supposed to have experienced. This account was totally lacking in detail. When the subjects were awoken from their trance state, they were asked to describe their experiences. Most individuals proceeded to unconsciously embellish the stories with details that they had not originally been given, thus demonstrating the role of the imagination in memory and recall. Given the incredible popularity of the imagery of the Greys, it is unsurprising that these people should have described their difficult experiences in these familiar terms.

The current belief in aliens and extra-terrestrials has reached a stage where it has become a kind of modern superstition. In many cases, these beings are portrayed as possessing incredible intelligence and powers beyond the scope of human comprehension, and so have come to resemble some kind of semi-deity.

In essence, these aliens seem to be fulfilling a role that has existed in man's subconscious for thousands of years. Today's aliens are really no different to yesterday's fairies, pixies, demons and monsters, a kind of throwback to our past that has been culturally updated for the technological age.

Although we may now inhabit a very different world from that of our ancestors, one in which we no longer need to be so fearful of the dangers of nature, people themselves remain unchanged and there is still that capacity in the human mind to create these fears and beliefs. Perhaps alien life forms, like the folk tales of yore, have arisen purely because the human mind has the capacity for fearful superstition?

And yet there is a small section of humanity that claims to have seen, met and even conversed with aliens. It is entirely possible, moreover, that these individuals are the privileged few to have been chosen by the extra-terrestrials for the purposes of contact with the human race. A curious form of intelligent life may have become aware of mankind's existence on Earth through its travels or perhaps as a result of our own emissions into the atmosphere in the form of rockets, probes or even television signals and radio waves and made its presence known.

Until the day when widespread contact with an alien civilization is irrefutably established, the debate over the existence of these extra-terrestrial beings will continue apace. Most of us will just have to wait and see.

MYSTERIES OF THE COSMOS

Since time immemorial, mankind has been questioning and studying the universe. Due to massive technological advances, we have now reached a stage where we can attempt to unravel some of the great mysteries, as scientific progress has given us the ability to venture into the vast unknown expanses of space.

Each step we take towards greater knowledge raises ever more difficult questions, some of which are bewildering in their complexity. Despite this, there are few people who do not believe that mankind's destiny lies beyond the confines of our own planet.

THE 1969 MOON LANDING

On 20 July 1969 the world watched in amazement as film footage depicted US astronauts Neil Armstrong and Buzz Aldrin taking their historic steps upon the surface of the Moon. As politicians and statesmen offered their congratulations to the USA, people all over the globe were inspired by this incredible feat.

It was called mankind's greatest achievement ever, and it was generally believed that it would usher in a new age – the space age – with Moon bases, space colonies and expansion through our solar system. Why then, several decades later, has none of this come about? Why has mankind not set foot on the Moon for over 40 years? Could the answer be that man never actually set foot on the Moon in the first place?

Almost as soon as the Second World War ceased, the USA and the Soviet Union started competing to land a man on the Moon. Both sides worked long and hard in their quest for victory, and seemed to have no qualms about utilizing the knowledge accumulated by Nazi scientists during the war to enable them to achieve their goal, as it was acknowledged that there was a great deal of political capital to be gained by the side that won.

The USSR enjoyed a series of advances, leading the way with the Sputnik programme and putting the first man, Yuri Gagarin, into space. For a considerable time, it seemed as if a Communist victory was inevitable, with the USA's space plan suffering a series of disastrous setbacks. Yet this was not to be, because it was the USA that, in the end, gloried in the moment of stepping on to the Moon's surface and planting its flag – or did it?

What was previously accepted as indisputable fact is now more frequently being viewed as a mystery – or even a conspiracy. Many experts who have studied the footage of the first Moon landing have suggested that it was, in fact, faked.

But was it really possible to fake the Moon landings and maintain the secret so successfully for so long? This would be a task almost as difficult as flying to the Moon itself, and it has to be said that no one claiming to have been involved in such a deception has ever come forward to expose it.

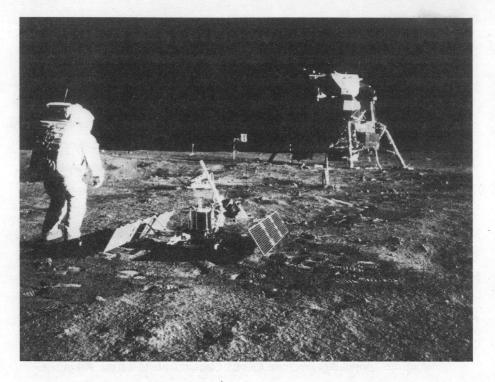

Apollo 11 astronaut Edwin 'Buzz' Aldrin deploys a scientific experiment package on the surface of the moon. In the background is the Lunar Module, as is a flag of the United States.

Nevertheless, there are many sceptics who still present some very convincing evidence for their arguments.

To start with, there are those who are suspicious of all the secrecy surrounding the space project, who view the restricted access to the facts as concealment of the evidence and a sure sign of conspiracy. All that we have as proof is the widely released footage of the two astronauts performing their tasks on the Moon surface, and it is this that has sparked most of the substantial allegations of deception. Many have claimed that there are enough errors and discrepancies in these images to illustrate the forgery convincingly.

The first, and most famous, of these concerns relates to the American flag. The footage depicts the astronauts planting the flag in the Moon surface and the 'Stars and Stripes' flapping wildly while they endeavour to keep it upright. What is peculiar is that, even after the flag has been firmly positioned, it continues to move as if it were blowing in the wind, an unlikely scenario in the light of the absence of any atmosphere on the Moon to cause such movement. Conspiracy theorists have argued that the motion of the flag was, in fact, caused by some kind of fan located within the photographic studio used to create the faked images. These claims have been countered by the suggestion that the moving flag may indicate that there is, after all, an atmosphere on the Moon, although, on the basis of established science, this seems highly unlikely.

Perhaps more difficult to dismiss so simply is the controversy relating to the surface of the Moon and the blast crater. The Apollo photographs clearly show that the lunar landscape is covered in a large amount of dust – this is obvious from the famous pictures of the astronauts' footprints and the later images of the tracks of the lunar rover. Samples of dust and rock were even put on display when the mission returned to Earth.

When the Moon lander came to rest on the surface of the Moon, it controlled its descent with a powerful rocket thruster which acted as a brake to stop it from crashing into the lunar surface. It stands to reason, therefore, that the photographs would be expected to reveal a large amount of displaced dust around the landing module and at least a small crater beneath it.

However, what is curious is that, on examination of the pictures of the lunar landing site, it appears that the lander has touched down without disturbing the lunar surface at all. There are no visible scorch marks anywhere and the area around the module seems undisturbed. The lander looks shiny and clean, with no trace of any settlement on its surface and even the module's feet are clean, despite sitting on large amounts of lunar dust.

A third point of contention in the lunar photographs is that relating to the shadows visible. While, on the Moon, there is only one light source – the sun – discrepancies in the shadows captured in these pictures suggest that more than one light source was, in fact, present. For example, some of the shadows of rock and objects can be seen to converge or cross, which should never happen if all of the light originates from one source.

In another image, Armstrong's and Aldrin's shadows appear to be of different lengths, again suggesting that more than one light source is being used. In one telltale shot, both astronaut and Moon lander are visible, with the sunlight illuminating them from one side.

The shot is particularly patriotic, for not only is the astronaut seen saluting the American flag, but he is also standing next to the lunar module that again displays the flag, as well as the words, 'United States'. The darkness of a lunar shadow should be pitch black, and yet the flag and words are highly visible on the dark side of the lander.

The conspiracy theorists argue that these irregularities with the lighting, and the movement of the flag, are evidence that the footage of the landings was not actually taken on the surface of the Moon at all, but rather, in a studio somewhere here on Earth. Further supporting this idea is the fact that in each of the photographs a peculiarly dark sky is visible, and yet, in the absence of any atmosphere on the Moon, the stars should have been especially visible from its surface.

Although the Moon landscape, the equipment involved and even the appearance of low gravity could all have been replicated by the film effects units of Hollywood, it would have been impossible to try to reproduce an accurate astrological representation of a starry sky.

It seems, therefore, that there may be evidence to suggest that man may not, after all, have landed on the Moon. And yet, even if this evidence were correct, it seems an improbable suggestion that man has not ventured into space at all. Global communications rely upon satellites that orbit the Earth at various altitudes and this would be impossible without space travel. Much of the work being done today in the fields of astrophysics and astronomy is conducted from orbiting telescopes such as the Hubble, which exist outside Earth's atmosphere. Once again, the technology required to put these instruments into space was developed in the space race that culminated in the Moon landings.

One cynical suggestion about the possible reasons for faking the Moon landings is that they were actually a politically motivated ruse to divert public attention away from the Vietnam War. During the run-up to the Moon landings, there was increasing opposition to the war, as well as a level of military failure. By landing on the Moon, the USA demonstrated victory, in scientific terms at least and, interestingly, the missions to land on the Moon ceased at around the same time as the war in Vietnam.

A completely alternative theory combines the ideas of conspiracy and deception. Based upon the belief that there are unusual artificial structures, and even cities, built on the Moon and perhaps also on Mars, it has been suggested that the publicly disseminated footage of the Moon landings was a cover for the amazing nature of what was, in fact, found there.

With the advances in technology that have taken place over the last few decades, there are few who doubt that mankind could not now fly to the Moon successfully. Whether, however, this was achieved back in 1969 is still doubted by some – in fact, it may require another trip to the Moon to prove that the flag still stands. Until that time, it seems likely that the satellite will remain a bewitching enigma, with space travel no more than a dream for mankind.

MOON CITIES

The two main theories put forward to explain the existence of mankind are, on the one hand, those that spring from religious notions of creation and, on the other, those that arise from scientific ideas, such as the process of evolution. A third theory is, however, gaining in popularity with many people all over the world, and they are awaiting further space exploration and technological advancement to prove them right. Their belief is that human life actually originated on a planet other than Earth, and has been in existence for much longer than is currently thought.

The discovery of the 'face on Mars' in 1976 – an apparent geological construction resembling human facial features – was greeted with great enthusiasm and sparked extensive research into the possibility of extra-terrestrial life within our own solar system. While many enthusiasts focused on examining the pictures of the Martian surface, others brought their attention to bear on other areas of our galaxy. Little did they expect such astounding discoveries.

Scientists such as Richard Hoagland, the American astronomer who pioneered this research, decided to examine the only other body of our solar system on which we possess any sort of detailed information, namely our Moon. In his close inspection of photographs of the lunar surface, Hoagland discovered several peculiarities that seemed to have been overlooked by the scientific establishment.

Clearly visible in some of the Moon photographs are structures that seem highly unlikely to have been formed by natural means. The first of these appeared in the Triesnecker and Ukert craters, which were created eons ago by meteor impacts. Within the radius of the Ukert crater is the unmistakable image of an equilateral triangle, one of the very foundations of geometry and almost impossible to explain as a natural phenomenon. Each side of the triangle is 26km (16 miles) long, and it can be viewed from Earth during a full Moon with just a small telescope.

Impressed by this remarkable discovery, astronomers scoured the existing lunar footage for more evidence of such anomalies. To many people, the existence of this triangular shape alone was evidence of some form of intelligent life and, if further proof could be found, then maybe a case could be made for looking for lunar inhabitants.

So, the examination of the lunar surface continued. All the areas of interest seemed to be located in that part of the Moon known to astronomers as the 'Sinus Medii' (Latin for 'Central Bay'). If one were observing a full Moon, this is the region around the centre of the visible disk. Within this area, in particular, investigators were drawn to a strange protuberance from the Moon's surface, known as 'the shard'. This geological feature is remarkable because it projects from the surface of the Moon to a distance of more than 1km (0.62 miles), in an otherwise sparse and flat landscape.

Perhaps the strangest of all formations to be detected on the lunar surface are those that appear in one of the photographs taken during the Apollo 10 mission. In frame number 4822, a structure can be discerned that appears to be floating just a few kilometres from the Moon's surface – this configuration is known as 'the tower' as it appears to have a cube-shaped top to it. Some sceptics have argued that this must be part of the mission probe's photo array, as such an object would defy the laws of physics. Others, however, are more willing to consider less conventional theories, and believe that this structure is strong proof of a former lunar city.

It is the latter group of people who are particularly interested in some of the other National Aeronautics and Space Administration (NASA) photographs, which appear to show large chasms in the lunar surface being spanned by a number of bridges. While this is not geologically impossible in itself, the proximity of such bridges to what have been described as ruined lunar cities may suggest that they were constructed artificially for the purpose of transport, rather than having arisen from any natural cause.

In examining these pictures, some people also claimed that the remains of a colossal dome are visible. It appears to contain a kind of grid pattern, suggesting that at some time it might have contained a lunar city. Using a system of dating based on the number of fresh impact craters in the area, it is estimated that the area that might have contained such a city has been ruined for around half a billion years.

Many people believe that the true extent of the lunar discoveries, as well as the evidence compiled from the surface of Mars, has been covered up by the government. They argue that the photographic footage released to the public has in some way been doctored to conceal the truth. These views, however, have been given no credence by scientists or by NASA, who attribute the objects themselves to quirks of geology and photographic defects.

Whatever the arguments, it seems safe to say that, as technology improves, it will not be long before people are able to use their own telescopes to look in ever greater detail at planets in our solar system, particularly the Moon and Mars.

It is likely that they will therefore soon be able to make their own judgements about these mysterious structures and their possible origins. It would certainly give mankind much to think about if any of these theories were proven to have their basis in fact after all.

MARTIAN CITIES

In recent years there has been much excitement over the notion that there may, indeed, be life on a planet other than our own and, in particular, on Mars. Various governments have pledged to launch an exploratory mission to Mars with the aim of landing a man on the planet, and this may well take place in the future. However, the majority of people who hope to find some evidence of present or past life on Mars expect this to be of the microscopic microbial variety, perhaps existing in a small amount of water beneath the planet's surface.

The expectation of the discovery of life on Mars received an unexpected boost in 1976, when mankind's first Martian probe reached the red planet. Named the Viking Orbiter 1, the probe's mission was to scan and map the surface of the planet, as this information was considered vital to scientists in their efforts to understand the mysteries of our planetary neighbour. The maps would also help them to choose a suitable location for the planned future landing of a mission to the planet in order to gather samples of the Martian surface for analysis.

When the scientists and astronomers involved in the project were examining the data from the Viking probe, they made a wholly unexpected discovery. In the Cynodia region of the planet there appeared to be a large hill, more than 1km (0.62 miles) wide, which in its formation unmistakeably resembled a human face.

After extensive investigation, the National Aeronautics and Space Administration (NASA) declared that the image was a purely chance formation, and that it had no real scientific significance. As such, the image was released to the public.

To many, however, this explanation was unsatisfactory, and the image generated great enthusiasm for the concept of life on Mars. Proponents of this idea have stated their belief that the Martian face is an artificial structure, created by some kind of intelligent life form. To build such a formation, its creators would have required knowledge and understanding of the physiology of the human face, and therefore it seemed that they were either humans themselves, or else they had come into contact with mankind at some point.

Further underpinning this theory are claims that a number of other features in the photograph could also represent artificial structures. For example, it has been suggested that several angular hills in the same Cynodia region were actually pyramids – if so, such a structure would provide an interesting link between our own world and the Martian environment. Unfortunately, the resolution of the photograph was too poor to be able to gain a conclusive answer either way.

Could it be possible that a civilization of humans, or at least one that was aware of humankind, had lived on Mars thousands of years ago? The debate continued, but the pictures had generated sufficient interest to warrant further investigation of the Cynodia region of the planet.

During the late 1990s and early 21st century, the Mars Global Surveyor was charged with making a sophisticated map of the Martian surface, and in 1998 and 2001 the orbiting satellite took a number of photographs of the disputed area.

At first it seemed that NASA's original verdict had been correct and the 'face on Mars' was simply a freak geological formation. Then, however, a fresh theory arose, which declared that the images revealed the existence of an entire city frozen beneath a Martian glacier near Mars' polar ice cap.

It seems that the information gleaned to date from the red planet is open to interpretation in a number of ways. Although there is a large base of established opinion ranged against the claims of life on Mars, many – such as American scientist Richard Hoagland – view the discoveries as evidence of a lost space culture that spanned our solar system, and perhaps even extended beyond it. Interestingly, even NASA agrees that it will take further investigations before the mystery is fully uncovered.

BLACK HOLES

Scientists have been trying to unravel the mystery behind the phenomenon known as the black hole for well over 100 years. No one has been able to offer any real proof that black holes exist; nonetheless, the existence of this dark force of the universe is largely accepted in theory, based upon the work of some of mankind's most brilliant minds.

It was in 1844 that the German astronomer Friedrich Wilhelm Bessel first postulated the existence of the black hole, based upon his observations of the 'dog star' Sirius. Sirius is the brightest star in the galaxy and Bessel was observing it through one of the most advanced telescopes of the day. He noted that, rather than moving in a straight line, as he would have expected, this star seemed to be subject to very slight undulations.

Bessel concluded correctly that this must be the result of some invisible force of gravity acting upon the star. Through the studies that he initiated, great discoveries have been made about the life stages of a star. For instance, it is now known that a star passes through four such stages in all, and at least 90 per cent of all known stars are thought to end up as black holes.

In the initial phase of a star's life, it is primarily comprised of the elements hydrogen and helium. Fusion takes place between the two elements, causing great energy to be released, and the entire nuclear process sees the build-up of immense gravitational forces at the centre of the star itself. A good example of a star at this stage of its life cycle is our own sun – the energy emitted by the sun is felt by us on Earth as radiation in the forms of heat and light.

As time passes and the fusion continues, the core of the star will grow continually denser, due to the fact that helium is a denser material than hydrogen, with a greater atomic mass. At the same time, the exterior layers of the star will expand and the star will grow in size. At this stage the colour of the light emitted will also change and the star will become classified as a 'Red Giant'. At the core of the star, immensely powerful reactions will still be taking place.

In the next part of the star's life, the outer layers of the Red Giant will gradually disperse until all that remains is the super-dense core. At this point, when it begins to emit a different wavelength of light, it is known as a 'White Dwarf'. It was when Sirius was in this phase of its history that it was spotted by Bessel back in the mid-19th century. Although, by today's standards, he was restricted in what he could see through his telescope, he noted that Sirius consisted of a pair of twin stars, and that the super-dense mass of one of the stars seemed to be affecting the other. It was only much later, with the advent of more advanced technology, that it was possible to see the light being emitted by the star in its 'White Dwarf' stage, and so begin to understand more fully what was happening.

Eventually, the star reaches its fourth and final life stage, represented by the concept of the mysterious black hole. This is formed when a 'White Dwarf' star collapses in on itself completely, and its matter becomes super-dense. The star is now millions of times smaller in size than when it started out, in contrast with its gravitational pull, which will be many millions of times greater.

Anything that comes into the gravitational range of the black hole will be drawn into it, whether this be planets, other stars, or even light. In fact, it is only because black holes draw light into them that scientists have been given any clue as to their existence. Although, without light, the black hole itself cannot be captured on film, what have been filmed are scenes showing matter being drawn into these pockets in space.

By using this method, astrologers are attempting to pinpoint the location of existing black holes within our universe.

Scientists have studied black holes and tried to suggest ways in which the enormous power of these peculiar facets of our universe could be harnessed in the future. Some maintain that they could hold the key to time travel, or to crossing large distances in space. Whether this is possible is not known, but what is guaranteed is that if any human being, on any kind of future space mission, were to stray anywhere near a black hole, it would spell certain death.

Others, such as the famous physicist Stephen Hawking, have postulated that black holes could actually provide humanity with a power source for the future, through the extraordinary energy they produce. It is unlikely that such a proposal would ever be met with anything other than resistance, however, as it would take only the smallest black hole to completely devour the entire Earth and, indeed, the whole solar system, meaning that there could be no margin for error whatsoever.

It would seem, according to the principles laid out in the theory of the 'big bang', that this is the eventual fate of the universe anyway. At present, the cosmos is still expanding as a direct result of the original 'big bang', but it is believed that the balancing force of this expansion will be its eventual contraction. Stars will collapse into black holes and the mass of these black holes will accumulate to incorporate whole galaxies, until the universe returns to the same state in which it started.

Whether scientists will ever succeed in making use of the awesome energy contained within the black hole is unknown – at the moment, certainly, it seems far too great a risk to contemplate seriously. Perhaps one day black holes will come to represent something other than an inconceivable power of destruction, but until that time they will be viewed with awe and wonder – and a great deal of respect.

WORMHOLES AND WARP DRIVES

Mankind has been fascinated by the notion of space travel for many years. The universe is a huge place, however, and we have to ask ourselves just how far it is possible for us to journey. Einstein's famous theory of relativity ($e=mc^2$) deems it impossible for a human being to travel faster than the speed of light and yet, if this is true, the vast expanses of space will remain forever inaccessible. Despite this, mankind still dreams of interstellar travel and many people believe that one day the human race will walk upon, and even colonize, alien planets. If this dream is to become a reality, one wonders how it will ever be possible.

To date, the farthest distance that human beings have explored lies just beyond the reach of our own solar system, a truly colossal distance of more than 6.5 billion miles (10.5 billion km). This journey was completed by two space probes, Pioneer 10 and Voyager 1. Launched in the 1970s, these probes have outlived their planned lifespan and explored farther than was ever expected.

However, even at the remarkable speeds at which these probes can travel, it would still take them many tens of thousands of years to arrive within reach of our nearest stellar neighbour. Our closest lone star is approximately 26 trillion miles (42 trillion km) or four and a half light-years away and those stars that have been linked to surrounding planets are many, many times further away than even this. By the time a probe reached its ultimate destination, humankind might no longer exist.

Current methods of space travel use a system of direct propulsion, involving igniting fuel and blasting a jet of it behind the craft to provide forward thrust. If this method were used for the purposes of interstellar travel, the amount of fuel required would be beyond the realms of the possible. There is also the problem of how to successfully control the great speeds at which any craft would have to travel as well as its means of deceleration and stopping. It is clear that if mankind is ever to journey to other star systems, a radical new approach to space travel will be necessary.

In pursuit of this, scientists have studied systems of nuclear fission as well as ion drives, but these have proved unfeasible. What has greatly interested researchers, however, in their search for entirely new possibilities in space travel is the use of warp drives and wormholes. While these cannot actually break the laws of physics, it is thought that they may be employed to bend, or ingeniously bypass, such constrictions.

Research into black holes has proved that space-time can be warped, and it is believed that, intriguingly, the fabric of space-time could be warped for the purposes of space travel.

The theory is that, by forcing the space-time behind a spaceship to expand, while simultaneously causing it to contract in front of the ship, the law of light speed could be conveniently side-stepped. Bizarrely, this would enable the spaceship to travel faster than the speed of light, without actually travelling through space at such a speed. In order to cause this warping effect, immense quantities of energy would need to be controlled very carefully.

An alternative method of space travel involves the creation of a wormhole – which is a hole in the very fabric of space-time itself. In laymen's terms, a wormhole amounts to the idea of folding space, bringing close together two places that are normally very far apart. For example, if there are two points on a map, A and B, the distance between them can be shortened immeasurably by folding the map so that A and B are touching each other, and are essentially in the same place. Physicists believe that it might be possible to do this with the concept of space-time.

The problem with this remarkably simple sounding theory centres around the enormous amounts of energy that would be required to turn such an idea into reality. The only forces that are capable of distorting space-time are immense quantities of mass and density, which produce huge gravitational power. To harness these we would need to learn how to manipulate the power of black holes and neutron stars. Even if we succeeded in mastering this technique, we would still need to learn how to control and navigate the space that we were using.

Although it is true that we have a great way to go before these ideas might become real possibilities, we have only to look at history for inspiration. For hundreds of years, suggestions that man might one day be able to fly were greeted with ridicule, as were notions of journeying to the moon or splitting the atom – however, these are all achievements that we now take for granted.

Unless we are prepared to allow the mysteries of the universe to remain unsolved forever, we must confront the incredible complexity of these matters with the same spirit that has led mankind to previous scientific victories.

INDEX